Discover the Real Jesus

DISCOVER THE REAL JESUS

BILL BRIGHT

Tyndale House Publishers, Inc.
WHEATON, ILLINOIS

Visit Tyndale's exciting Web site at www.tyndale.com

Discover the Real Jesus

Portions of this book were adapted from Bill Bright, *Transferable Concepts for Powerful Living* (San Bernardino, Calif.: Here's Life Publishers, 1985) and Bill Bright, *How You Can Pray with Confidence* (Orlando: NewLife Publications, 1998). Used by permission. All rights reserved.

Designed by Ron Kaufmann

Edited by Lynn Vanderzalm and Michal Needham

Library of Congress Cataloging-in-Publication Data

Bright, Bill.
  Discover the real Jesus / Bill Bright.
    p. cm.
Includes bibliographical references.
  ISBN 0-8423-8620-3 (pbk.)
  1. Jesus Christ—Person and offices. I. Title.
BT203.B75 2004
232—dc22   2004008296

Printed in the United States of America

10 09 08 07 06 05 04
 8   7   6   5   4   3   2   1

The Bright family lovingly dedicates this book to the Campus Crusade for Christ International staff, who are committed to helping people around the world discover the real Jesus. Their lives faithfully demonstrate Jesus' love and forgiveness as they enthusiastically share these truths. By their lives and their words they are truly helping to change the world.

CONTENTS

ACKNOWLEDGMENTS

God graciously allowed Bill enough time to complete *Discover the Real Jesus* before he discovered Jesus in heaven. It was my joy to share fifty-four years, six months, and twenty days of married life with a man who loved Jesus passionately and served Him faithfully.

Bill depended on the integrity of men and women who helped in the research and editing of his manuscripts. John Nill and Helmut Teichert recognized the challenge to accomplish Bill's goals, and they have moved forward with strength of purpose to complete the projects Bill felt God wanted him to do. Brenda Josee listened carefully to Bill's final content and instructions for this book about the most important person who ever lived. She has captured Bill's passion for Jesus and his desire for everyone to know Him personally.

Tyndale House Publishers continues to be a great blessing as they promote The Legacy series of books. Editors Joette Whims and Lynn Vanderzalm have handled the manuscript in a most professional manner.

Bailey Marks, Ted Martin, and Gordon Klenck agreed to review the manuscript on Bill's behalf, and I trust these men completely. They worked closely with Bill for more than four decades and observed closely Bill's love and commitment to the real Jesus.

It is my prayer that the person of Jesus Christ will become very real to every reader.

Mrs. Bill Bright (Vonette)

AN INCREDIBLE MAN

I have a friend who's had an amazing impact on my life. Maybe you have a friend like that too.[1]

This man is the epitome of integrity. In the midst of a culture where too many people live by deception and the power of unbridled egos, my friend is true to the core. What you see is what you get. He has no pretense, no show. He is utterly reliable. When he says he'll do something, he does it. It's so refreshing. I know I can trust this man.

I have such confidence in my friend's wisdom that when I have key decisions to make, he's the person I turn to. He's a patient listener, helping me to explore my options, my motives, and my doubts. He has given me advice countless times in my life, and never once has that advice led me in the wrong direction.

Our relationship is so comfortable that I tell him everything and anything. He makes me feel safe. He lets me dream, always encouraging me to press on to accomplish big things for God. He also lets me unearth the dark parts of my heart, the doubts and fear, the insecurities and temptations. When I do that, though, he never attacks me. He listens, and then in his gentle way he prods me to change, always pointing me toward what is true and pure.

And he's like that with everyone he knows. Patient. Kind. Wise. True.

One of the things I most admire about him is his compassion. He is so sensitive to people's needs. While he cares for people of every stripe and background, he has a real heart for the poor. He's the kind of man who spends time with homeless people, with Alzheimer's and AIDS patients, with the people society often casts aside as worthless. But no one is worthless to him. I've seen him give attention and value to people most of us would ignore or avoid. He's as comfortable with a convict as he is with a church leader. I wish I had his heart and love for people.

That's really the crux of it for me. This man is so attractive that I want to be like him. I want his heart. His humility. His ability to love sacrificially. His absolute commitment to the truth.

My friend has been a powerful mentor to me. As I said, I just want to be more and more like him.

As you've probably guessed by now, the friend I describe is Jesus Christ. He's everything I've said about him—and more. So much more. I've written this book because I want you to meet Jesus for yourself.

My hope and prayer is that you will discover who Jesus really is. And when you do, your life will be changed forever.

I didn't always know and love Jesus. In fact, I entered adulthood very confident in my own skills and power. I didn't need anyone else.

Let me tell you my story. . . .

---

[1] Even though Dr. Bright died during the final revisions and editing of this book, the publishers decided to retain the verb tenses in the present tense to reflect his thoughts in his initial writing of the book.

PART 1

Who Is Jesus?

~

My purpose is to give you life in all its fullness.

JESUS

1

A Momentous Decision

*W*hen you look back at your life, can you point to one event that changed your entire future? I vividly recall a day that upended almost everything I believed.

The day started out innocuously enough. I was a young man at the time, starting a new adventure. I had just moved to Los Angeles, the movie capital of the world, from a ranch near Coweta, Oklahoma. I had dreams of becoming a successful actor or businessman so that I could be wealthy, live in a big house, drive the best cars, and travel the world. The teeming culture of Southern California seemed like the place to achieve my goals.

I came from an ambitious family. My grandfather, Samuel Bright, had made the "run for land" during the land-rush days in Oklahoma in the late 1880s. My father, Dale Bright, was a macho rancher who could ride wild broncos and tame unruly cattle. These two men were my role models. They were honest, hardworking, and unafraid. I expected to be as successful as they were.

On my first day in Los Angeles, I stopped for a red light at the corner of Sunset Boulevard and Figueroa Street, where I noticed a clean-cut young man looking for a ride. When I asked him if he wanted to jump into my car, he introduced himself as Dawson Trotman. Later, I found out that he was the director and founder of the Navigators evangelistic ministry. He invited me home for dinner, and since I was so new in town and had nowhere else to go, I accepted.

Around the Trotman dinner table, I met some other people associated with the Navigators organization. These people were intelligent, attractive—and they quoted Bible verses!

This combination was a mystery to me. As a youngster in Coweta, I had been baptized and had joined the local church, but those were rituals most people observed. My grandfather and father considered religion all right for women and children, but the men in my family were not too involved in the church. In fact, for them the church was a part of the community's social fabric, nothing more. Since I wanted to be like the men in my family, especially my grandfather, I accepted their perspective.

After dinner at the Trotmans', the men announced that they were going to a birthday party at the home of Charles E. Fuller in honor of his son, Dan, who was home from the navy. Our country was in the midst of World War II, and I had ardently wanted to join the military, but a pierced eardrum barred my enlistment. When the men asked if I would like to come along to the navy man's birthday celebration, I accepted.

At the party, I met another group of appealing people who were also very open about their religious beliefs. They talked about Jesus Christ as if they knew Him. But they didn't press me about my beliefs. After the party, I stayed overnight at the Trotman home, then went on my way.

About that time, I became involved in a business partnership making and selling specialty food. Within a short time, I bought out my partner and worked eighteen- to twenty-hour days building Bright's California Confections. My products were picked up by several well-known stores and even marketed overseas. At the same time, I was studying drama at the Hollywood Talent Showcase, doing amateur radio once a week, and in my spare time riding horseback in the Hollywood Hills. I had money for clothes and a nice car. The future looked sunny.

SHAKEN FROM MY PATH

Right about that time another unusual event happened. I rented an apartment from a friendly elderly couple who repeatedly invited me to attend their church. They were excited about their pastor, Louis Evans Sr., and I was mystified about how anyone could love a preacher so much.

Late one Sunday afternoon when I was returning from riding in the hills, I impulsively decided to check out my landlord's church, Hollywood

Presbyterian. I slipped into the back pew because I smelled of horse and sweat. I left before the service ended, deciding that I had done my duty.

Not too long after that, I received a call from a young woman involved in the church's college and career department. She invited me to attend a party at a ranch owned by a movie star who was a member of the church. Of course, I agreed to go. Meeting a rancher who was an actor might be a good connection for my own acting career.

I didn't know what to expect at this sort of a party, but what I saw surprised me—three hundred of the sharpest college-age men and women I had ever met. Their happiness didn't fit the mold of my ideas about religious people. And strangely, they also talked about Jesus Christ as if they had truly met Him.

Attracted by what I saw, I started attending church meetings. Soon I got to know Dr. Henrietta Mears, a tireless worker and dynamic woman who was the education director at the church. She had traveled the world and had a global perspective on life. She shattered all my preconceived ideas about what a religious person was. She talked to our group about a living, personal God who wanted to have a relationship with each person He had created. This captivated me.

My confusion over religion came to a head one Wednesday evening in the spring of 1945. Dr. Mears was teaching from the New Testament about the life of the apostle Paul. She told us the story of how he zealously tried to stamp out the new religion that had recently cropped up. That religion was what we today call Christianity. In the early part of his life, Paul's goal was to capture Christians so that he could take them to Jerusalem, where they would be stoned. He was a true anti-Christian zealot.

But as Paul (then known as Saul) traveled to Damascus one day, an amazing moment changed his life forever. Right there on that road, Paul was blinded by a brilliant light, and he heard a voice that called his name and asked, "Why are you persecuting Me?"

Confused by the mysterious voice, Paul asked, "Who are you?"

The voice answered: "I am Jesus, the One you are persecuting! Now get up and go into the city, and you will be told what you are to do" (Acts 9:5-6).

From the moment Paul heard that voice, his life was changed. Jesus Christ had pursued him and cared enough to stop him in his tracks.

Paul's life did an about-face. Soon he began preaching and teaching about Jesus, the very one he had hated, and Paul became instrumental in establishing a new movement that in time would spread around the globe!

When Dr. Mears finished telling the story, she addressed her audience. "The happiest people in the world," she explained, "are those who are in the center of God's will. The most miserable people are those who are not doing God's will."

Her words hit me hard. I thought of my own ambitions and goals—they were all self-centered. I had not considered God when making any of them.

But what Dr. Mears said next was even more earthshaking. "Not many of us have dramatic emotional conversion experiences as Paul did. But the circumstances don't really matter. What matters is your response to the questions 'Who art Thou, Lord?' and 'What wilt Thou have me to do?'"

Then she challenged us to take the next step by going home, getting on our knees before God, and asking Him the same two questions.

That night I did exactly what she suggested. I knelt beside my bed and asked with a prayerful heart, "Who art Thou, Lord?" and "What wilt Thou have me to do?" I didn't have an emotional experience or hear directly from Jesus as Paul did. But at that moment, I began my personal journey in discovering the real Jesus Christ. Little did I know how much those questions would change my life![1]

RELIGION OR RELATIONSHIP?

Since that night more than fifty years ago, I have found that many people have a serious misconception about Jesus Christ—they see Christianity as a religion, not a relationship. This is the difference: Religion is our effort to reach up to God. In other words, we feel we must do "this" and "this" and "this" to obtain God's attention and pleasure. Christianity, however, is the story of how God reached down to begin a relationship with us. He did this by sending His perfect Son, Jesus Christ, to open a way for us to have a deep and meaningful relationship with the God of the universe.

When humans invent a religion, they create a god in their own image—gods made of wood or stone or metal. Museums around the world are filled with the images of gods who resemble the people who worshipped them. The character of the gods reflects the culture in which they were conceived.

But Jesus came to a world that was not expecting someone with His character and mission. Even His closest friends didn't understand what He was about until after His death. In the person of Jesus of Nazareth—a Jewish man who ministered along the dusty roads of the Middle East for about three years—God reached out to His human creation. This contact was personal and loving, and it culminated in the greatest sacrifice ever made.

My dear friend Josh McDowell, who has probably spoken to more audiences about the claims of Christ than anyone else in history, tells the story of how he had fallen into the trap of thinking that Christianity is a religion. Josh was a brash, self-centered university student when he found himself attracted to a group of students who had a quality he desired. During a conversation with a group of them, he asked, "What makes you different?"

One young woman in the group looked Josh straight in the eyes and said, "Jesus Christ."

"Don't give me that kind of garbage," Josh exclaimed. "I'm fed up with religion, the Bible, and the church."

The woman shot back, "Mister, I didn't say 'religion.' I said 'Jesus Christ.'"

Josh went on from that day to meet the Person who *is* Christianity—Jesus Christ. And Josh's life was radically changed.[2]

DISCOVERING THE REAL JESUS

In this book I want to introduce you to the real Jesus—the Person who desires to have a relationship with you. Of course, as we discover who Jesus is, we will have to look at some facts about His life, His death, and His mission on earth. But these facts are a way of understanding the personality and love of Jesus and His desire to be your closest friend.

I can tell you from personal experience that *knowing* Jesus—not just knowing *about* Him—will change your life in ways you cannot imagine. Perhaps you have already met Him in a personal way but are seeking to understand Him more deeply. Or maybe you have never been introduced to Him on a personal level and want to know more.

Jesus is the most attractive person you will ever meet. After five decades of walking with Him, I can tell you that His qualities have come to mean so much to me: His unconditional love when I fail Him; His patience when I don't "get it" very quickly; His compassion when my heart aches; His joy when my whole world seems to be crumbling. As you read along with me, you will find in Jesus qualities that will become meaningful to you too. He's like that. He touches each of our lives in ways that are unique to our personality and circumstances.

Getting to know Jesus will change how you interact with the world. Years ago when I was a small boy, I remember watching my father break in wild horses. How skilled he was! He took plenty of time and patience to get the bridle over the quivering nostrils of the animal. As I watched, I could see that my father knew just how to handle the unruly creature so that the horse could become a useful part of the ranch. So many times I have thought about that scene and related it to how patient and gentle Jesus has been with me all these years as He has worked with my outlandish thoughts and behaviors. He had a lot to change in the heart of that vain, ambitious young Oklahoma man who was out to conquer the world.

Another vivid picture I have of my father is when he would tame a wild colt. He would bring the young animal's mother into the corral to stand beside him. Eventually, the colt would calm down and inch close to his mother. Gradually, my father would move between the colt and the mare, and the colt would allow him to slip on the bridle. The colt could be tamed because he saw the acceptance in his mother's eyes.

This, too, reminds me of Jesus. He is the One who stands beside us, full of wisdom and calmness. He is there to protect us, to teach us, to show us what is good and what to avoid. He has much more concern for our lives than the mare had for her colt.

THE ADVENTURE BEGINS

My grandfather and my father are still two of the most important role models in my life. Although both of them have died, my memories of them are clear and endearing. My mother's faith also remains as a dominant force in my life. Her influence grew as I became more aware of her love for Jesus.

But beginning on that spring day in 1945, I found someone who is the perfect role model. That person is Jesus Christ. As I grew closer to Him, my commitment to His mission grew deeper. And I became more like Him in every way.

In the coming pages I want to share with you just how He took the raw clay of a materialistic young man and gave me a life of adventure that I never could have imagined. He showed me not only who He is but also what He wants me to do.

But right now, these questions hang in the air for you to answer: Who do you say that Jesus is? and What does He want you to do? Until you answer these questions, your life will not be complete. In the next chapter, we will tackle the issues behind these questions.

Before we go on, let me explain about the "Discover Jesus" questions that you will find at the end of each chapter. I encourage you to take time to consider each question asked there. They will help you relate the concepts in the chapter to your own unique life situation.

Read about the Real Jesus: Listen to what the apostle Paul said later on in his life:

> I harshly persecuted the church. And I obeyed the Jewish law so carefully that I was never accused of any fault. I once thought all these things were so very important, but now I consider them worthless because of what Christ has done. Yes, everything else is worthless when compared with the priceless gain of knowing Christ Jesus my Lord.
>
> PHILIPPIANS 3:6-8

1. What things were very important to Paul, and why did he later consider those very things to be worthless?

2. What things do you consider to be "so very important" in your life?

3. On a scale of 1 to 10, how would you rate your knowledge about Jesus? (1 = next to nothing, and 10 = I've learned everything there is to know about Him)

4. On a scale of 1 to 10, how would you rate your desire to know more about Jesus? (1 = no interest at all, and 10 = great interest)

2

"Who Do People Say
That I Am?"

I shared my story in the last chapter. But what about you? What's your story? What do you know about Jesus?

Even more important than what you know *about* Jesus, do you know Him personally? Or does that question sound odd to you? Does it seem strange to be able to know God's Son personally?

Let me ask you this: Is Jesus an appealing person to you? Is He someone you want to get to know?

Or think about this: Where did you learn what you know about Jesus? From friends? from your family? from books and movies? Were your sources reliable? Can you trust what you hear about Jesus? What about now?

It's my observation that our culture is quite confused about who Jesus is. Much of our society dismisses Him as irrelevant, many people relegating His name to expletives or profanity. In America we have not only passed laws that prohibit the invocation of His name in our schools, but we have also allowed personal peace and material affluence to distract us from the Person who claims to be the Prince of Peace. As a result, for many people Jesus is little more than a cultural icon—no different from any other religious leader.

If you were to ask people on the street who Jesus is, you would hear a variety of answers:

Ron, a thirty-year-old computer programmer, says, "He's one of the most influential people in history, of course, but I don't buy the idea that He was anything more than that. He said some important things, but that doesn't make Him God." People like Ron see Jesus as a significant teacher, but they don't think His life and teachings have an ultimate impact on them.

Erika, a graduate student in psychology, says, "I respect your belief in Jesus, but the whole Christianity thing doesn't make sense to me. I've always found my truth in Tao, but recently I've been looking into motherwave. It's basically all the same." Erika's response is interesting because it reflects the view of many people in our world, especially postmodernists. They assert that all beliefs are essentially the same. They say, "I have my truth, you have yours, but nothing is true for every person for all time and in all places. Jesus Christ is just some people's option for truth."

Or take Jack, a businessman whose net worth is in the seven figures. "Who is Jesus? Frankly, I don't think too much about it. I can see how Jesus is helpful for some people—for the poor, for people who don't know any better. But I have education, my business, a great wife, and two daughters who are doing well at Ivy League schools. I just don't need Jesus. I'm doing quite well without Him."

Do you see yourself in any of these responses? Do you know people who are confused about who Jesus is?

Interestingly, uncertainty about Jesus is not new. Even the people who knew Him during His time on earth were confused. The New Testament records an incident when Jesus was with His disciples, the twelve men who were closest to Him. While they were relaxing one day, Jesus asked them a startling question: "Who do people say that the Son of Man is?" (Matthew 16:13).

The disciples clearly understood that Jesus was asking about Himself. Perhaps they hesitated to answer, wondering if they should tell Jesus about all the rumors they had heard about Him. Some might have been afraid to give the wrong answer. But they did reply. "Some say John the Baptist, some say Elijah, and others say Jeremiah or one of the other prophets" (v. 14).

Their answers showed how confused the people were about Jesus. Evidently most people agreed that Jesus was a unique person, but was He a prophet, a teacher, a spiritual leader? Or was He just a crackpot who had a following?

After Jesus listened to their answers to His first question, He then asked an even more probing question: "Who do *you* say I am?" (v. 15, emphasis added).

This was the heart of the matter. Jesus had taught His disciples about

God, performed miracles in their presence, shown them His nature. Were they getting the message?

Peter, the impetuous disciple, spoke up first. "You are the Messiah, the Son of the living God" (v. 16).

That was it! Peter had understood!

Jesus responded to Peter's bold declaration with these words: "You are blessed, Simon son of John, because My Father in heaven has revealed this to you. You did not learn this from any human being" (v. 17).

So, I ask you the question Jesus asked His followers: "Who do you say that I am?" Are you confused, like Ron, Erika, and Jack? Or are you confident, like Peter?

A BOLD CONFESSION

I remember a confident, clearheaded confession of who Jesus is from a surprising source. A number of years ago I heard one of the intellectual and diplomatic giants of the twentieth century speak. Dr. Charles Malik earned his doctorate at Harvard University and was awarded fifty honorary doctorates from universities such as Toronto, Harvard, Yale, Princeton, Columbia, and Boston. He held professorships in philosophy at several leading universities in America, Canada, and Lebanon, the country of his birth. Charles Malik's books about philosophy, diplomacy, human rights, and international affairs became authoritative in their respective fields. He signed the United Nations Charter for Lebanon in 1945 and served in the United Nations for fourteen years. He was named president of the U.N. General Assembly and the Security Council.

I mention these details to emphasize the stature of Dr. Malik. In an address to a group of esteemed world leaders, he said:

> Only those who stay close to Jesus Christ can help others who are far away. The needs of the world are much deeper than political freedom and security . . . much deeper than social justice and economic development, much deeper than democracy and progress. The deeper need of the world belongs to the sphere of the mind, heart, and spirit, a spirit to be penetrated with the light and grace of Jesus Christ. . . . I really do not know what will remain of civilization and history if the accumulated influence of Jesus Christ, both direct and indirect, is eradicated from literature, art, practical dealings, moral standards, and creativeness in the different activities of mind and spirit.

Dr. Malik concluded his address with these inspiring words: "The heart of the whole matter is faith in Jesus Christ."[1]

I was so moved by Dr. Malik's words that I approached him to express my appreciation for his convictions about Jesus Christ. I told him, "Many political leaders speak of God, the Bible, and prayer in a general way, but I have never heard one in your position of worldwide leadership speak so powerfully and so convincingly of his faith in and love for Jesus Christ."

He replied, "I am sobered by the words of our Lord." Then he quoted Matthew 10:32-33: "Whosoever therefore shall confess me before men, him will I confess also before my Father which is in heaven. But whosoever shall deny me before men, him will I also deny before my Father which is in heaven" (KJV).

Charles Malik was confident of who Jesus is. He was a true disciple of Jesus, one who unashamedly followed his Master into the busy and conflicting crossroads of modern life in the university, the marketplace, and the chambers of diplomacy. He was a role model I could follow. It was my privilege to have counted him as a friend for nearly twenty-five years before he died in 1987.

GETTING ANSWERS

If you are not confident like Charles Malik, if you are more like Ron or Erika or Jack, how will you get answers to the questions of who Jesus is and what He wants you to do? Where can you get reliable information?

Today, people learn about Jesus in various ways. As children, they may have attended Sunday school or church services where they heard Bible stories about Jesus. Some people base their knowledge of Jesus on what they have seen in movies or on television.

Some people rely on information gleaned from conversations around the office watercooler or from material found in textbooks. I've known many students whose knowledge of Jesus came from teachers and professors who were antagonistic to Christianity.

Our culture tries to give clues about Jesus, but even those are confusing. During the celebration of Jesus' birth, He often gets upstaged by Santa, and during the Easter holidays, the message of Jesus' sacrificial death for us is overshadowed by the Easter bunny and spring fashion.

So, where does a person go to get reliable information? How can a person separate what's true from the myths that have sprung up about Jesus?

One way we get to know Jesus is through a method we often use to get to know other people: by learning what other people say about that person, especially the person's closest friends.

WHAT DID JESUS' FRIENDS SAY ABOUT HIM?

The first four books of the New Testament—the Gospels of Matthew, Mark, Luke, and John—are written by followers who knew Him close-up. These historical accounts give us the closest look at Jesus' life. We see Him in action, we hear what He says, and we watch Him interact with all kinds of people: teaching them, healing them, and pointing them to His Father.

The Gospel of Matthew records one of the first statements a person made about Jesus' adult life. John the Baptist, the man chosen to prepare the world for Jesus' ministry, said of Him: "I baptize with water those who turn from their sins and turn to God. But someone is coming soon who is far greater than I am—so much greater that I am not even worthy to be His slave" (Matthew 3:11). On the day John baptized Jesus, God the Father announced who Jesus is with these words: "This is My beloved Son, and I am fully pleased with Him" (Matthew 3:17).

Matthew also chose to record some of Jesus' most profound teachings: the Beatitudes, teachings about anger, adultery and divorce, revenge, loving our enemies, giving to the needy, prayer, as well as money and possessions (see Matthew 5 and 6). We can learn a lot about who Jesus is by listening to His teaching about these practical issues.

The Gospel of Mark records the words of a Roman officer who watched Jesus die. The officer said, "Truly, this was the Son of God!" (Mark 15:39). This man had a clear picture of who Jesus is.

Along with the other Gospel writers, Luke recorded many occasions on which Jesus healed people, forgave their sin, and performed some remarkable miracles.

John, the beloved disciple of Jesus, said of Him, "No one has ever seen God. But His only Son, who is Himself God, is near to the Father's heart; He has told us about Him" (John 1:18).

The disciple Peter begins one of his letters, "I am writing to all of you who share the same precious faith we have, faith given to us by Jesus Christ, our God and Savior, who makes us right with God" (2 Peter 1:1). Peter wrote these words many years after he answered Jesus' question, Who do you say that I am? Peter's letter shows that he never changed his opinion about who Jesus is. Instead, his commitment and devotion to Jesus grew year after year.

In the letters the apostle Paul wrote, he tells us many things about who Jesus is. For instance, in Romans Paul says Jesus is the person who:

- *Gives us eternal life—as a free gift:* "For the wages of sin is death, but the free gift of God is eternal life through Christ Jesus our Lord." (Romans 6:23)
- *Takes the punishment for our sins and makes us right with God:* "For God sent Jesus to take the punishment for our sins and to satisfy God's anger against us. We are made right with God when we believe that Jesus shed His blood, sacrificing His life for us." (Romans 3:25)
- *Makes us friends of God:* "So now we can rejoice in our wonderful new relationship with God—all because of what our Lord Jesus Christ has done for us in making us friends of God." (Romans 5:11)
- *Gives us peace with God:* "Therefore, since we have been made right in God's sight by faith, we have peace with God because of what Jesus Christ our Lord has done for us." (Romans 5:1)
- *Will never condemn us:* "Who then will condemn us? Will Christ Jesus? No, for He is the One who died for us and was raised to life for us and is sitting at the place of highest honor next to God, pleading for us." (Romans 8:34)

Are you getting a glimpse of who Jesus is? His friends say some remarkable things about Him.

THE IMPACT OF WHAT PEOPLE SAY ABOUT JESUS

I hope that you are becoming increasingly eager to discover the real Jesus. I'm always excited to see that once people know the truth about Jesus, their lives change in amazing ways.

I remember one situation in which the words that Jesus' friend John said about Him transformed a most unlikely person. While I was speaking to a group of several hundred students, a young man rose to challenge what I said. He began criticizing me for encouraging students to turn their lives over to Christ. I didn't know who he was, but he was very upset that I was saying that Christ and His teachings are the answer to America's cultural and social problems.

Rather than argue or debate with the young man in front of the crowd, I concluded my remarks and spoke to him afterward in private. "I resent your effort to convince these students to become Christians," he said. "You have no right to impose your views on them. You are older and more mature than they are, and they are like putty in your hands."

I discovered that he was head of the Communist party on campus and was no friend of religion. His goal as head of a radical student organization was exactly the same as mine: to influence students ideologically. He didn't see the double standard he was using in trying to keep me from influencing students for Christ while he tried to sway them toward Communism.

I invited him to come home with me for dinner so that we could continue our conversation. He accepted, and we had a delightful evening. He was a brilliant and articulate young man, engaging in every way. By the time we finished our meal, we had become friends. I discovered that the source of his reaction to my remarks was the same as it is with so many who reject Jesus. He was rejecting a religious system but had never considered the Person of Christ.

I knew that if this radical young man knew the real Jesus, he would have difficulty rejecting Him, the most radical person who ever lived. I told the young man I would like to read to him some passages from the Bible.

He reacted strongly. "I don't believe the Bible. I don't want to hear anything you read. I've read the Bible from cover to cover, and it's filled with contradictions and myths. I don't believe a word of it!"

Over his objections, I read from the Gospel of John in *The Living Bible*. "Before anything else existed, there was Christ, with God. He has always been alive and is Himself God. . . . Eternal life is in Him, and this life gives light to all mankind. His life is the light that shines through the darkness—and the darkness can never extinguish it" (1:1-5).

I read several more verses, then concluded with this verse: "Christ became a human being and lived here on earth among us and was full of loving forgiveness and truth. And some of us have seen His glory—the glory of the only Son of the heavenly Father!" (1:14).

The young man leaned forward abruptly and asked to see the passages I had just read. He read them over thoughtfully and handed the Bible back to me without a word. I then turned to Colossians 1 and read verses 13-20.

[God] has rescued us out of the darkness and gloom of Satan's kingdom and brought us into the Kingdom of His dear Son, who bought our freedom with His blood and forgave us all our sins. Christ is the exact likeness of the unseen God. He existed before God made anything at all, and, in fact, Christ Himself is the Creator who made everything in heaven and earth, the things we can see and the things we can't; . . . All were made by Christ for His own use and glory. He was before all else began and it is His power that holds everything together. . . . It was through what His Son did that God cleared a path for everything to come to Him—all things in heaven and on earth—for Christ's death on the cross has made peace with God for all by His blood.

The young man's reaction was the same. Again he asked to see the text I had read. Some time passed as he appeared to be reading the verses over and over. When he handed the Bible back to me, I turned to Hebrews 1. Again, I read a description of Jesus, how He was God's way to relate to us and how He did this by shedding His blood.

At this point, I felt as if I was in the presence of a different young man. His hard edge, his belligerence and antagonism were melting away. He was hearing things he had never heard or at least had never taken seriously before. To conclude, I turned to 1 John 2:22-23 and read: "Who is the greatest liar? The one who says that Jesus is not Christ. Such a person is antichrist, for he does not believe in God the Father and in His Son. For a person who doesn't believe in Christ, God's Son, can't have God the Father either. But he who has Christ, God's Son, has God the Father also."

When I finished reading, we chatted for a while longer and ended an enjoyable evening. As he prepared to leave, I asked if he would sign our family guest book. Later I noticed that he had written the words, "The night of decision!"

A young leader who just hours before had stood boldly to condemn Christianity as a religion had met Jesus Christ. All that was necessary for him to change his view was to come face-to-face with the real Jesus.

That's the secret for you too—getting to know the *real* Jesus. Not the one expressed in stereotypes created by misinformed people. Not the one seen in many movies and on television. Not the one often paraded for our religious holidays. But the real Jesus. The one who loves you and wants to have a relationship with you. The one who makes you a friend of God. The one whose death took away all your guilt and shame. The one who wants to give your life meaning and purpose.

Read about the Real Jesus: Let's look again at the passage mentioned in the early part of this chapter:

> [Jesus] asked His disciples, "Who do people say that the Son of Man is?"
>
> "Well," they replied, "some say John the Baptist, some say Elijah, and others say Jeremiah or one of the other prophets."
>
> Then He asked them, "Who do you say I am?"
>
> Simon Peter answered, "You are the Messiah, the Son of the living God."
>
> Jesus replied, "You are blessed, Simon son of John, because My Father in heaven has revealed this to you. You did not learn this from any human being."
>
> MATTHEW 16:13-17

1. Are you confident or confused about who Jesus is?

2. If Jesus asked you today, "Who do you say I am?" what would you say?

3. What does Peter's response—"You are the Messiah, the Son of the living God"—mean to you?

4. How did you arrive at your current beliefs about Jesus? What were your sources?

5. What will you do and where will you go to get to know Jesus better?

3

What Does Jesus Say about Himself?

*I*t is interesting to read what Jesus' close friends and followers said about Him; however, it is much more significant to be aware of what Jesus said about Himself.

When you are introduced to someone new—a neighbor, an acquaintance, or a coworker—you naturally go through a certain process to get to know that person. Think back to the last time you met new people. You found out their names and a few facts about their lives. You may have asked about their families, their interests, and you began to assess their character. Are they shy or outgoing? intellectual? practical? humorous? Where do they like to spend their leisure time?

As you make a personal connection with these people, you decide if they are compatible enough with your personality to become close friends. If your relationship deepens, you discover more intimate details of their personalities. What are their deep hurts and joys? How has their background affected their outlook? What goals do they have for their lives?

How do we learn about Jesus? Let's listen to what He says about Himself.

IN HIS OWN WORDS

On one of the early days of Jesus' ministry, He went to the synagogue at Nazareth. Somber scribes, prestigious religious leaders, and devout laymen patiently waited to hear the Word of God read aloud as was the custom on the holy day.

The synagogue attendant brought out a sacred old scroll containing a part of the Bible written hundreds of years before by the prophet Isaiah. He opened it carefully. Jesus, the carpenter's son, was chosen to read.

This is what Jesus said: "The Spirit of the Lord is upon Me, for He has appointed Me to preach Good News to the poor. He has sent Me to proclaim that captives will be released, that the blind will see, that the downtrodden will be freed from their oppressors, and that the time of the Lord's favor has come" (Luke 4:18-19).

When Jesus finished reading, He rolled up the scroll and handed it back to the attendant. Every eye watched as He sat down. Confidently He looked around and announced, "This Scripture has come true today before your very eyes!" (4:21).

The people were amazed at who He had just claimed to be. They knew Him as Joseph's son, the carpenter who lived in Nazareth. Yet He had just indicated that He was God's sent One, the promised Messiah. "How can this be?" they asked (4:22).

What kind of man would dare to make those declarations? How could He prove that outrageous claim?

Jesus of Nazareth made many startling statements about Himself. He declared that He was God: "The Father and I are one. . . . Anyone who has seen Me has seen the Father!" (John 10:30; 14:9). He said that His words were eternal: "Heaven and earth will disappear, but My words will remain forever" (Mark 13:31). He also asserted that He had divine authority: "I have been given complete authority in heaven and on earth" (Matthew 28:18). Amazing.

I Am

One of the unique ways Jesus described Himself was as the "I AM." His Jewish listeners understood clearly what He meant when He made that claim. Many years ago, God had spoken to Moses through a burning bush in the desert. This is what God said of Himself at that time: "I AM THE ONE WHO ALWAYS IS" (Exodus 3:14). This phrase can also be translated as "I AM WHO I AM." In other words, God *is*. He has no limits. He is everything at once. He is God over all. Nothing limits God.

The name I AM was sacred to the Jewish people. (Today, we know the name as Jehovah or Yahweh.) This name for God summed up all that God was and is. The Jews would not even spell out the name Yahweh because they considered it so holy.

Then Jesus came, and He claimed to be the I AM. "I tell you the truth," Jesus answered, "before Abraham was born, I am!" (John 8:58, NIV). Not only did Jesus claim to be alive before the time of Abraham, but He also took on Himself the holy name of God, Yahweh. His Jewish listeners were aghast. This was blasphemy in their eyes, so they took up stones to kill Him right there in the Temple. But Jesus slipped out of their sight.

Jesus made other "I am" statements about Himself. He said

- *I am the bread of life:* "I am the bread of life. No one who comes to Me will ever be hungry again. I am the true bread from heaven. Anyone who eats this bread will live forever and not die as your ancestors did." (John 6:35, 58)
- *I am the light of the world:* "I am the light of the world. If you follow Me, you won't be stumbling through the darkness, because you will have the light that leads to life." (John 8:12)
- *I am the gate:* "I am the gate for the sheep. . . . Yes, I am the gate. Those who come in through Me will be saved. Wherever they go, they will find green pastures." (John 10:7-9)
- *I am the good shepherd:* "I am the good shepherd. The good shepherd lays down his life for the sheep. . . . I know My own sheep, and they know Me." (John 10:11, 14)
- *I am the resurrection and the life:* "I am the resurrection and the life. Those who believe in Me, even though they die like everyone else, will live again." (John 11:25)
- *I am the way, the truth, and the life:* "I am the way, the truth, and the life. No one can come to the Father except through Me." (John 14:6)
- *I am the vine:* "I am the true vine, and My Father is the gardener. . . . You are the branches. Those who remain in Me, and I in them, will produce much fruit. For apart from Me you can do nothing." (John 15:1, 5)

These are truly astounding claims, and they do not allow us to be neutral about who Jesus is.

WHAT WILL YOU DO WITH JESUS?

I could add many other claims that Jesus made, but these are enough to show that Jesus was no ordinary man. We have two choices: we can believe that He is the Son of God, or we can believe that He is deluded. He doesn't leave us any other options. In his famous book *Mere Christianity*, C. S. Lewis makes this plain:

> A man who was merely a man and said the sort of things Jesus said would not be a great moral teacher. He would either be a lunatic—on the level with the man who says he is a poached egg—or else he would be the devil of hell. You must take your choice. Either this was, and is, the Son of God; or else a madman or something worse. You can shut Him up for a fool . . . or you can fall at His feet and call Him Lord and God. But let us not come with any patronizing nonsense about His being a great human teacher. He has not left that open to us.[1]

My purpose for writing this book is to give you a glimpse into the life, death, and resurrection of Jesus Christ so that you, too, can know that He is God—more than a mere man. In part 1, I have introduced you to a few of the claims that Jesus' friends made about Him as well as claims that Jesus made about Himself.

Part 2—"Why Is Jesus So Important?"—will show you how Jesus' life and death prove His claims and make a way for us to have a deep and fulfilling relationship with Him. We will also find out why the world has reacted to Jesus the way it has and how the life of someone who lived so long ago is so vital to us today.

Part 3—"How Do I Respond to Jesus?"—will take what we have learned about Jesus and discover what that all means to our lives. What does He expect of me? If I decide to become one of His followers, what should I do? These chapters will explain what I learned so many years ago—that Jesus will change your viewpoint, your actions, and your attitudes, all for the better. Your life will never be the same.

Part 4—"How Do I Spread My Love for Jesus?"—will outline practical ways we can use what we have learned in the rest of the book to help others around us. After all, the Bible tells us that Jesus came to the whole world, not just our little corner. Putting these plans into action will transform how we relate to others and the joy we experience.

I'm so glad that you are taking this journey with me to discover the greatest man who ever lived. Whether you feel you know quite a bit about Jesus or are not sure what He is about, you will enjoy the trip. I can say with all the fervor of my heart that knowing Jesus and being close to Him for more than fifty years has been my most exciting adventure. With Him, I never knew what to expect around the corner of life, but what I experienced by the side of Jesus was more than I ever imagined. I am sure that you, too, will find your greatest satisfaction in knowing Jesus.

Discover Jesus

Read about the Real Jesus: Look again at one of the "I am" statements Jesus made:

> I am the way, the truth, and the life. No one can come to the Father except through Me.

JOHN 14:6

1. Jesus says He is the way. The way to what?

2. How have you been trying to find your way to God? Have you been successful?

3. Where do you find truth in your experience?

4. How do you respond when you hear Jesus say that He is the truth? Are you willing to trust that Jesus is who He says He is?

5. From what you've learned about Jesus in this chapter, how can He give you life?

PART 2

Why Is Jesus So Important?

~

God did not send His Son into the world to
condemn it, but to save it.

JESUS

4

The Miraculous Birth

*W*hy are people so fascinated with the Christmas story? What elements of Christmas are meaningful to you? During the holiday season, store windows are filled with crèche displays, loudspeakers peal out Christmas carols, and Christmas trees are hung with lights and angels. Even though our world tries to hide the religious significance of the season beneath commercialism and secular symbols, most people still realize that Jesus' birth is the underlying reason for our holiday celebrations.

The story of Christmas is filled with amazing details. Imagine how excited Mary must have been when Joseph first asked her parents for her hand in marriage. Although the Bible doesn't say much about Joseph, it does give us a picture of a man who came from a decent family, had skills as a carpenter, and who was probably hardworking and devoted—a good young man.

According to the customs of that day, Mary and Joseph would have agreed to a year of betrothal before their marriage. A betrothal was much like an engagement—with one big difference: it was a binding agreement that could be severed only by a decree of divorce. During this time, the two people would prepare for their life together. After the period of betrothal, the couple would consummate their marriage and begin living as husband and wife.

Surely Mary's heart was singing in anticipation of her future. She was young and had many fulfilling days ahead of her. She would marry, accomplishing the dream of young women in that culture.

Then one day Mary's life was upended. God sent the angel Gabriel to give her a message: "Greetings, favored woman! The Lord is with you!" (Luke 1:28).

Mary was confused. Why would an angel speak to her? She was no one important—just a young woman living in Nazareth, an insignificant village in Galilee.

What the angel said next took her breath away. "Don't be frightened, Mary, . . . for God has decided to bless you! You will become pregnant and have a son, and you are to name Him Jesus. He will be very great and will be called the Son of the Most High. And the Lord God will give Him the throne of His ancestor David. And He will reign over Israel forever; His Kingdom will never end!" (Luke 1:30-33).

Can you imagine how the angel's words must have sounded to this simple village girl? She would carry the Messiah? Her confusion only deepened, so she asked the angel, "But how can I have a baby? I am a virgin" (Luke 1:34).

Then the angel gave Mary one of the most astounding statements God has given to anyone: "The Holy Spirit will come upon you, and the power of the Most High will overshadow you. So the baby born to you will be holy, and He will be called the Son of God. . . . For nothing is impossible with God" (Luke 1:35, 37).

This was more amazing than anything Mary had heard before. She would have a baby whose conception would be unique in all of history. Jesus would have no biological human father! The Holy Spirit would implant the seed of the child in Mary's womb.

Are you wondering what purpose God had in intervening in the life of this ordinary woman? Why would He select someone so unimportant and poor? If baby Jesus would someday rule the world, why wasn't He born in a palace?

In fact, this birth was the event that God had planned before He created the world. The prophets had foretold it in Old Testament times. Through Jesus, God was carrying out His plan to bring all people into a relationship with Him.

THE MYSTERY OF GOD'S PLAN

What was Mary's reaction to this astounding news? Her response shows why God selected her to carry the Christ child: "I am the Lord's servant, and

I am willing to accept whatever He wants. May everything you have said come true" (Luke 1:38).

Most likely Mary understood part of what her role in this miraculous plan would cost her. She lived in a tight community that would be aghast when it learned Mary was pregnant before she was married. What would Joseph think? Would he refuse to marry her, thinking that she had been unfaithful to him? But she considered those problems small compared to the joy of obeying God.

God made sure that Mary was cared for. When an angel told Joseph God's plan for Mary, Joseph continued with his plans to marry her. He, too, was willing to obey God.

Then more problems arose. Just when Mary was nearing the time of her delivery, the Roman government ordered all Jewish males to travel to their ancestral home to pay a tax. Imagine what Mary and Joseph must have felt. Now they would be burdened with an added tax and a long trip from Nazareth to Bethlehem, the home of King David, Joseph's ancestor. The trip must have been a hardship for Mary, who was in her ninth month of pregnancy.

When they arrived in Bethlehem, Mary and Joseph were greeted by masses of people threading through the streets. All the inns were booked! Didn't anyone care about a young expectant mother who badly needed rest? What a dilemma for Joseph, who knew Mary needed a warm bed and special care. But the only place he could find was a corner in a stable. He settled her in, and the labor pains began.

Why would God allow this to happen? The serene nativity scenes we see portrayed today do not convey the real-life hardships of having a baby in an animal stall or placing a newborn in a food trough because there were no other facilities. Did Joseph feel like a failure? Was Mary discouraged?

Yet this was the humble birth that God had chosen for His Son. No servants waiting on Jesus. No specially prepared cradle. No cooing grandparents hovering over Him.

A ROYAL ANNOUNCEMENT

The birth of the Christ child was a humble event that went unnoticed in the hustle and bustle of Bethlehem. Men bringing their animals to the stable probably did not even give the young family a second glance. The innkeeper who owned the stable probably forgot about Mary and Joseph in his rush to serve his paying customers.

But God knows the hearts of all people. He saw some grubby, lowly shepherds in the fields guarding their flocks of sheep. Like Mary and Joseph, they were commoners whom no one noticed. But they were given the most incredible news that night: The Messiah was born in Bethlehem!

A choir of angels announced the news. At first the shepherds were frightened, but then they accepted the message with joy. They said, "Come on, let's go to Bethlehem! Let's see this wonderful thing that has happened, which the Lord has told us about" (Luke 2:15). They ran into the village, jostled their way through the crowds, and found the baby in the manger. They were so excited about what they witnessed that they told everyone they met about the birth of the Messiah!

Mary and Joseph and the shepherds had angels to tell them about Jesus' miraculous birth. But how do we know for sure that the Christmas story is true?

Perhaps this story has raised some questions in your mind. Why did Jesus have to be born? Why did God choose a virgin birth? How do we know for sure that Jesus was the One sent from God?

WHY DID JESUS HAVE TO BE BORN?

Indian Thicke was a member of the high caste in India. He had a profound sense of the reverence of life and would not kill an ant or a cobra or a cow because he believed in reincarnation and felt he might be killing some relative. When he heard that Jesus was God, he could not comprehend how the great God of the universe could become a man and why He would do this. Then one day when he was walking in a field, meditating on this new truth about Jesus and wondering how this could possibly be, he came upon a large anthill.

He observed with wonder and amazement the activity of the ants. Suddenly, he heard the noise of a tractor plowing the fields and realized that the tractor would soon plow through that anthill. Thousands of ants would be killed and their home destroyed.

He became frantic. How could he warn the ants? He thought, *If I write in the sand, they wouldn't know how to read the message. If I shout, they would not hear me. The only way I can communicate with the ants is by becoming an ant myself.* Suddenly, he understood why the Creator of the universe chose to become one of us!

Just as Thicke would have needed to become an ant to communicate effectively with the ants, so God became a man to communicate the danger of sin and the need for repentance and faith to humanity. Central to the idea of God's becoming a man is what theologians call "the incarnation of Christ." The word *incarnation* comes from the Latin root *carne*, meaning "flesh." The doctrine of incarnation asserts that Jesus Christ is "God in carne"—God in human flesh.

God's desire is to have a personal relationship with His children. To do that, He had to open a way for us to communicate with Him. Through Jesus' birth, we see

- What God is like through the physical life of Jesus;
- That God understands what it's like to be a fragile human in a fallen world;
- That Jesus loves us so much that He was willing to sacrifice His glory in heaven for us; and
- That we can approach God through Jesus.

Jesus' birth enables us to relate to God. No longer is He only that magnificent being sitting on a throne in heaven, but He is also that baby Mary held in her arms.

Think of what this birth meant for Jesus. He had lived from eternity in heaven, a place of absolute joy and beauty. Angels constantly worshipped him; He had no limitations or pain.

Then He put all that aside to be born as a baby in a stable. Paul describes the sacrifice of Christ's human birth: "Though He was God, He did not demand and cling to His rights as God. He made Himself nothing; He took the humble position of a slave and appeared in human form" (Philippians 2:6-7).

Earlier we said that religion is human effort to reach up to God. We could never lift ourselves to God's level of perfection and sinlessness. The birth of Jesus, on the other hand, shows how God came out of heaven into our harsh world to begin a relationship with us! The world had never before seen such sacrifice and such love.

WHY DID GOD CHOOSE A VIRGIN BIRTH?

Think about the physical characteristics you've inherited from your parents or even your grandparents. Maybe you have your mother's green eyes and your father's dark hair, but you got your height from your grandfather. What other traits were passed on to you? Do you have your dad's gift for making people laugh? Do you tend to procrastinate like your mom?

Not only do we inherit physical characteristics and personality traits from our parents, but we also inherit a sinful nature at birth. Since Adam and Eve sinned in the Garden of Eden, the sinful nature has been passed from one generation to another. It's not hard to find evidence of the sin nature. For example, is it easier for a small child to hoard his toys or to share them with a friend? This sin tendency is part of our inner being.

The Bible says that all people have a sinful nature. This means that our natural bent is toward doing what's wrong and selfish. "For all have sinned; all fall short of God's glorious standard" (Romans 3:23). We can recognize this fatal flaw in our own lives and in the actions of people everywhere. How easily do you get irritated and short-tempered when you are under pressure? How generous are you with your money when you see someone in need? What are your thoughts when you see sexual scenes on television?

However, our sin comes with a consequence. We will discuss this in more detail in chapter 7, but let me summarize here. The Bible tells us that "the wages of sin is death" (Romans 6:23). In the Old Testament, God required that an animal without a blemish or defect be sacrificed to pay for sin (see Deuteronomy 17:1). In the New Testament, God offered His only Son, Jesus Christ, as the spotless sacrifice for our sin. "He paid for you with the precious lifeblood of Christ, the sinless, spotless Lamb of God" (1 Peter 1:19). What role does Christ's virgin birth play in that? The Virgin Birth provided for us One who did not inherit a sinful nature. Because He was conceived of the Holy Spirit and is God, He lived a sinless life. He is spotless. Through His payment for our sins' wages, He opened up the way for us to begin a dialogue with a holy God.

HOW CAN WE BE CERTAIN JESUS IS THE ONE?

I'm sure you've heard angry teenagers say, "I wish I had never been born into this family!" Other people have commented, "I wish I had been born with a silver spoon in my mouth." None of us chose any of the details of our own birth. An amazing fact about Jesus' birth is that He is the only One who chose His place of birth, His family, and the circumstances into which He was born!

How do we know this? God did not just spring His plan to save humankind on the world without giving prior notice. All through the Old Testament, the prophets told about the coming of the Messiah, the sent One from God who would take away the sins of the world. These prophecies were given hundreds of years before Jesus was born.

Jesus is the only person who existed before His conception and birth—He has always existed. He therefore could orchestrate the details of His birth. Look at the chart to see how accurately the prophets foretold of Jesus' birth and how exactly Jesus fulfilled them![1]

Old Testament Prophecies	Details of Prophecies	Fulfillment in Jesus
Genesis 12:1-3	Messiah would be a descendant of Abraham	Matthew 1:1-2 Luke 3:23, 34
Genesis 49:10	Messiah's descent through the tribe of Judah	Luke 3:23, 33
Micah 5:2	Messiah's birth in Bethlehem	Luke 2:4-7
Daniel 9:25	Time of Messiah's birth	Luke 2:1-2
Isaiah 7:14	Messiah's virgin birth	Luke 1:26-31
Isaiah 9:7	Messiah, the heir to David's throne	Luke 1:32-33
Jeremiah 31:15	Slaughter of Jewish children when Messiah was a child	Matthew 2:16-18
Hosea 11:1	Messiah's family's flight to Egypt to escape death	Matthew 2:14-15

Space does not allow a complete analysis of prophecies concerning the birth of Christ, but the eight listed above are typical of the accuracy of all Old Testament prophecies. Peter W. Stoner, a professor of mathematics and astronomy, explains the probabilities of eight prophecies being fulfilled in one person: "We find the chance that any man might have lived down to the present time and fulfilled all eight prophecies is 1 in 10^{17} of being absolute [in mathematical terms, 10^{17} = one hundred quadrillion or 100,000,000,000,000,000]."

To describe how remote a possibility this number represents, Stoner suggests that, after laying one hundred quadrillion silver dollars two feet deep across the state of Texas, we mark one of them and stir the whole mass thoroughly. We blindfold one man and ask him to pick up one silver dollar from anywhere in Texas, but he must pick up the marked coin. The probability of his retrieving the exact one is the same likelihood that the prophets had of writing these eight prophecies in their human understanding and of having them all come true, in any one man, from their day to today.

"Now these prophecies were either given by inspiration of God," says Stoner, "or the prophets just wrote them as they thought they should be. In any case, the prophets had just one chance in 10^{17} of having them come true in any man, but they all came true in Christ."[2] And that's not even considering the odds against the other hundreds of prophecies that Jesus fulfilled in detail!

A CHANGE OF VIEW

Still, many people have difficulty believing that Jesus is the Son of God. As a new believer, I was apprehensive that some great archaeologist might reveal shocking evidence that would challenge my belief that Jesus is truly the Son of God. But as only God could do, He used someone to assure me of the truth of Christianity.

Dr. Cyril E. Joad was one of the world's leading intellectuals. Head of the Department of Philosophy at the University of London during the mid-twentieth century, he was one of England's most colorful and controversial figures. A pacifist and an agnostic, Dr. Joad authored forty books on philosophical, intellectual, and cultural issues of his day. He was a colleague of leading agnostic and atheistic figures, such as historian H. G. Wells, philosopher-mathematician Bertrand Russell, biologist Sir Julian Huxley, and playwright George Bernard Shaw. With them, Dr. Joad staunchly supported rationalism and anti-spiritualism.

Throughout most of his life, Dr. Joad publicly denied the Virgin Birth and the deity of Christ. Instead, he believed that Jesus was only a man, that God was part of the universe, and that if the universe was destroyed, God would be destroyed. Dr. Joad also believed that sin didn't exist and that humankind was destined for utopia. With just a little more time, humans could achieve heaven on earth. In their day, Dr. Joad and his colleagues probably did more than any other group to undermine the faith of college students.

Then events changed Dr. Joad's viewpoint. Two world wars and the threat of a third world war demonstrated beyond any reasonable doubt to this brilliant scholar that humankind was sinful. All he believed was under suspicion.

In 1953, with sudden and great conviction, Dr. Joad reversed his views and became a zealous follower of Jesus. Because he wanted to atone for his former evil influence that had caused many people to reject Christ, he wrote the book *My Return to Faith*. This book opened many hearts and minds to the claims of Christ.

Dr. Joad's words also had an influence on me. As I studied and prayed, I became convinced that the Christmas story was factual and inspired. God had indeed stepped into our world through the Virgin Birth. One of the titles Jesus is given is *Immanuel*, which means "God with us." That is the essence of the miraculous birth of Jesus!

Because Jesus was born of a virgin through the supernatural power of the Holy Spirit, He could be God and man at once. The two natures of Christ—divine and human—are one of the mysteries of the ages. Understanding what this means will give us the ability to know how God relates to us and how we can relate to Him.

Discover Jesus

Read about the Real Jesus: Compare these two passages about Jesus:

From the Old Testament: The Lord Himself will choose the sign. Look! The virgin will conceive a child! She will give birth to a son and will call Him Immanuel—"God is with us."

ISAIAH 7:14

From the New Testament: All of this happened to fulfill the Lord's message through His prophet: "Look! The virgin will conceive a child! She will give birth to a son, and He will be called Immanuel (meaning, God is with us)."

MATTHEW 1:22-23

1. How sure are you that the Christmas story happened exactly as the Bible says it did? What difference do the details make?

2. How do you celebrate Jesus' birth? Do your holiday celebrations deepen your faith or contribute to commercialism?

3. What does the statement "God is with us" mean to you?

4. If Jesus is truly present with us today, how will that change how you live your daily life?

5

The Mystery of Two in One

$\mathcal{E}$ric enrolled in a college several states east of his home city. Since he knew no one at the university, he met his roommate for the first time when he moved into the dorm. Randy wore a cowboy hat and boots and spoke with a Texas drawl. Right away Eric could tell that Randy was a nice person but that his new roommate didn't have much in common with him.

The next two weeks proved Eric's first impression correct. Randy listened to country music, while Eric enjoyed jazz. Randy liked the local steak house; Eric's favorite was Chinese cuisine. Randy pursued a humanities degree, while Eric was deep into higher mathematics. The two of them didn't even have classes in the same buildings. But Randy and Eric worked out an amiable living arrangement and went their own ways outside the dorm.

One day Eric and a classmate, Lisa, went to the student union to work on a project. When they entered the main door, they noticed huge posters on easels announcing a student art exhibit in one of the conference rooms the next weekend. Lisa stopped to read the details.

Eric stood behind her, not all that interested until his eyes fell on a familiar name on the poster. It was Randy's! His art was being featured in the exhibit.

When Eric got back to his dorm room, he looked around with new eyes. On the wall above Randy's bed were some watercolor paintings that Eric had seen but had never paid attention to before. As he looked at them closely, sure enough, he found Randy's signature inconspicuously tucked into a corner. The paintings were wild with color and pulsated with desert heat.

When Randy came in, Eric began questioning him about his art. Randy's eyes came alive as he described his artistic vision. Eric felt embarrassed. Here he had lived with this person for months and never realized how much talent his roommate had. What else was hidden under the cowboy hat and drawl? There was much more to Randy than he had first thought.

I sometimes wonder if the disciples had a similar experience when they met Jesus. What they saw at first was a man—even though they realized He was unique and sent from God. But they didn't understand all that lay beneath the flesh and blood of the man they had chosen to follow. Over the course of three years of spending time with Him, they discovered a truth that wasn't evident at first sight—Jesus was God in the flesh!

The disciples came to believe this amazing truth: Jesus has two natures—God and man—at the same time. He is the only person who could ever make this claim. What does it mean that Jesus was both divine and human? How did He demonstrate this fact?

TWO NATURES IN ONE

Understanding the uniqueness of Jesus Christ's most astounding quality is difficult but essential. Jesus is wholly God, but He is also completely human. Let me give you two Bible verses that confirm this fact:

- *Jesus is fully God:* "In Christ the fullness of God lives in a human body." (Colossians 2:9)
- *Jesus is fully human:* "Look at My hands. Look at My feet. You can see that it's really Me. Touch Me and make sure that I am not a ghost, because ghosts don't have bodies, as you see that I do!" (Luke 24:39)

These verses and many others in the New Testament teach that Jesus is God and human *at the same time.* He is not half God and half man. Nor is He composed of two persons, one divine and the other human. Rather, Jesus Christ is *one* person with *two* natures. These two natures of Christ are inseparably united without mixture or loss of their individual identities.

Perhaps this is a difficult concept for you to understand or accept. You are not alone. Christians over the centuries have wrestled with the meaning of Christ's two natures. Yet as we learn more about Jesus, we will see that His divinity and His humanity are both essential for the work He came to earth to do. If He had not been fully God and fully man, He could not have accomplished His mission from God.

Theologians have a term for Christ's two natures—*the hypostatic union of Christ*. The phrase comes from the Council of Chalcedon, a famous church council that met in AD 451. The members discussed Christ's nature and released this statement:

> [Jesus is] consubstantial with the Father as to his Godhead, and consubstantial also with us as to his manhood; like unto us in all things, yet without sin; as to his Godhead, begotten of the Father before all worlds; but as to his manhood, in these days, born for us men and for our salvation, of the virgin Mary, the mother of God, one and the same Christ, Son, Lord, only-begotten, known in two natures, without confusion, without conversion, without severance, and without division; the distinction of the natures being in no wise abolished by their union, but the peculiarity of each nature being maintained, and both concurring in one person and subsistence. We confess not a Son divided and sundered into two persons, but one and the same Son, and only-begotten, and God-Logos, our Lord Jesus Christ.[1]

The editors of the *Tyndale Bible Dictionary* comment on this explanation: "In theological parlance it has become customary to speak of the union of the divine and the human in the Person of the incarnate Redeemer as the 'hypostatic' union (*unio hypostatica*), from the Greek word for 'person.' It is important to note not only *that* the union is personal, but also *why* it is so. Theologians speak of the union as personal because it is the act of a Person, namely the Son of God, the Word who became flesh."[2]

Admittedly, it takes a theologian to unpack all the meaning in the council's statement. But since then, many esteemed Christian thinkers, councils, and other groups have reaffirmed the hypostatic union of Jesus. To summarize what these illustrious people meant, we could say this: At His unique birth, Jesus took upon Himself a human nature and remains both undiminished deity and true humanity united in one person forever. This is part of God's perfect plan to reach down to His human creation and set

up a way we could understand and communicate with Him forever—
through Jesus!

While the deity and humanity of Jesus are one united whole, for our own
understanding we will consider each separately. This will help us gain a
clearer picture of the two natures of Jesus.

Was Jesus Really God?

A person would naturally think that the president of a seminary would
have the clearest views about Jesus. But that isn't always true. Years ago I
had the opportunity to meet the president of one of America's most prestigious seminaries. When I came to see a friend who was studying at the seminary, he introduced me to the school's president and mentioned that I was
the president of Campus Crusade for Christ.

Realizing that I had spent many years working with college students,
this gentleman asked me, "Mr. Bright, when you talk to college students
about becoming a Christian, what do you tell them? Better still, what
would you tell me? I'd like to become a Christian."

I was stunned. This man was known for his position at the head of a
Christian school! And yet here he was admitting that he didn't know Jesus.

"As a result of my research into the life of Jesus," he explained, "I began
to rethink my views about Him. Now I'm convinced that no honest person
who is willing to consider the overwhelming evidence proving the deity of
Christ can deny that He is the Son of God."

Then he asked me something I will never forget because the tone of his
voice deeply moved me. "Will you help me know Jesus as my personal
Savior?"

I prayed for him; then he prayed. My student friend also prayed. That day
one of America's great scholars began a relationship with the Son of God.

The facts proving that Jesus is the Son of God are irrefutable. Consider
these:

- He performed all kinds of miracles, including healing diseases,
  calming storms, and raising people from the dead.
- He knew more about God and heaven than any normal person could
  know.
- He fulfilled Old Testament prophecy concerning His birth, life,
  death, and resurrection (see Isaiah 7:14; Zechariah 9:9; Isaiah 9:1-2;
  53:3-12; Psalm 16:10).

- His wisdom astounded all who heard Him (see Matthew 7:28-29; 22:15-46).
- He predicted future events, including His own death and the destruction of the Temple in Jerusalem (see Mark 8:31; Matthew 23:37–24:2).[3]

Furthermore, God's Word clearly identifies Jesus as fully God. Paul writes a compelling testimony in Colossians 1:15-17: "Christ is the visible image of the invisible God. He existed before God made anything at all and is supreme over all creation. Christ is the One through whom God created everything in heaven and earth. He made the things we can see and the things we can't see—kings, kingdoms, rulers, and authorities. Everything has been created through Him and for Him. He existed before everything else began, and He holds all creation together."

This passage shows us that Jesus *is* God. Because God is spirit, we cannot see Him. But Jesus became God in the flesh so that we could know God. Imagine the Creator of the human body agreeing to live within that creation of flesh!

The writer of the book of Hebrews explains Jesus' divinity like this: "Long ago God spoke many times and in many ways to our ancestors through the prophets. But now in these final days, He has spoken to us through His Son. God promised everything to the Son as an inheritance, and through the Son He made the universe and everything in it. The Son reflects God's own glory, and everything about Him represents God exactly" (Hebrews 1:1-3).

These verses are crystal clear—Jesus is God. Jesus is the voice, the hands and feet, the eyes and ears of God in the flesh. In fact, the religious leaders of Jesus' day didn't seek to kill Him because He had a big following or because He preached a different theology. They wanted Him to die because He claimed to be equal with God the Father: "So the Jewish leaders tried all the more to kill Him. In addition to disobeying the Sabbath rules, He had spoken of God as His Father, thereby making Himself equal with God" (John 5:18).

But the event that proved without question that Jesus is God was His resurrection. No other person in the universe can claim to have defeated death, then live forever afterward. This fact is so central to who Jesus is that we will take time in a later chapter to examine what His resurrection means to the world—and to you and me.

Was Jesus Really Human?

Once a visitor came to tour the campus of a small college. Since he was alone and unfamiliar with the layout of the grounds, he approached a man who was energetically scrubbing walls in a classroom building. "Do you know where I can find the office of the college president?" he asked.

"Yes," the workman said as he rinsed his sponge in a bucket of soapy water. "He should be in his office by noon." Then he pointed the visitor to the right building and went back to work.

Two hours later, the visitor returned and easily found his way to the correct building. A secretary escorted him into the office of the president. To the visitor's surprise, behind the mahogany desk sat the workman, now dressed in a suit and tie!

The two men enjoyed a brief conversation; then the visitor went on his way. The following day, a letter arrived for the college president. Inside the envelope was a grant for thousands of dollars and a note from the benefactor: "You were not too proud to do the most menial task in order to improve your school, and I want to invest in your efforts."

The humble investment this college president made for the sake of his school was nothing compared to what Jesus did for us! Have you thought of how much He gave up to become a man? Can you imagine the humility it took for Jesus to walk among people who hated Him and called Him names? Here are some facts that prove His humanity:

- He was born of a woman (see Matthew 1:16).
- He had a body made of flesh and blood (see Hebrews 2:14).
- He hungered (see Matthew 4:2).
- He wept in prayer (see Hebrews 5:7).
- He grew thirsty (see John 19:28).
- He got tired (see John 4:6).

Have you ever been so bone tired that you could hardly move a muscle? Jesus experienced that over and over. If you read through the four Gospels (Matthew, Mark, Luke, and John), you will see how often people crowded in on Him, demanded His attention, and complained about what He was doing. He walked hundreds of miles during His three years of ministry. He climbed mountains and descended into valleys. He rode in fishing boats. He preached and taught and prayed for the people He met. Wherever He went, He had the twelve disciples beside Him. He had taken on the responsibility of training them and getting them ready to carry on His ministry. Many times they even looked to Him for basics such as food and rest.

But one more fact absolutely proves that Jesus was a man: He died. Just as the Resurrection proves the deity of Jesus, the death of Jesus assures us that He is human. The story of the Crucifixion is the crux of what Jesus came to do for us—the suffering, the pain, and the torment that led to our salvation. Later we will look more deeply into the details that make the death of Jesus so miraculous and humbling. But this is what we glean from His two natures: Just as the death of Jesus is merely a tragedy without His resurrection, the humanity of Jesus cannot have meaning without understanding His divinity. Just as the death and resurrection of Jesus are one in the miracle of our redemption, the humanity and divinity of Jesus are one in the miracle of Christ's nature.

Perhaps you still have questions about how Jesus could be fully God and fully human at the same time. No one can completely understand this mystery of God. We will further explore the nature of Jesus in the next chapter by looking at how He ministered while He walked on earth. How Jesus spoke, interacted with people, and displayed emotions all stayed true to His character and showed both His deity and His humanity. This look at the real Jesus will warm your heart and thrill your soul!

Read about the Real Jesus: Think about the two natures of Jesus:

> **Jesus is the Son of God:** The angel replied, "The Holy Spirit will come upon you, and the power of the Most High will overshadow you. So the baby born to you will be holy, and He will be called the Son of God."
>
> LUKE 1:35

> **Jesus is the Son of Man:** Then Jesus began to tell them that He, the Son of Man, would suffer many terrible things and be rejected by the leaders, the leading priests, and the teachers of religious law. He would be killed, and three days later He would rise again.
>
> MARK 8:31

1. How has your view of Jesus changed since you learned about His two natures?

2. How does the title *Son of Man* help you understand and relate to Jesus?

3. How does the title *Son of God* change how you listen to what He says?

4. Which of Jesus' two titles means the most to you in a situation you are facing right now?

6

Our Good Shepherd

*B*orn in Yugoslavia in 1910, Agnes Bojaxhiu responded to God's call on her life when she was still a teenager. She was appointed to work in the city of Calcutta, India, with its teeming masses of sick and starving. While there, one sight revolutionized her life—a homeless woman dying in the gutter while rats gnawed the woman's body. Compassion compelled the young Yugoslavian to beg for an abandoned Hindu temple from the government, which she converted into a crude, makeshift hospital for the dying. This statement became her life's mission: "If there is a God in heaven, and a Christ we love, nobody should die alone."[1] The goal of the woman who would come to be known as Mother Teresa was to share the compassion of her Savior, Jesus Christ. Eventually she established colonies for ten thousand lepers in twenty-eight cities. Her work brought her worldwide fame. She received the Nobel Peace Prize in 1979 and was named "Most Admired Woman" by *Good Housekeeping* magazine.

BBC News commentator Malcolm Muggeridge interviewed this woman. He asked her, "Mother Teresa, the thing I noticed about you and the hundreds of sisters who now form your team is that you all look so happy. Is that a put-on?"

She replied, "Oh no, not at all. Nothing makes you happier than when you really reach out in mercy to someone who is badly hurt."[2]

Unquestionably, Mother Teresa is one of the outstanding figures of the twentieth century. The love, grace, and care she showed to countless hurting people throughout her life provides one of the greatest examples of the tender compassion Jesus had for the suffering and lonely. Mother Teresa tried to emulate Him in her ministry to the grief-stricken poor of India.

THE GOOD SHEPHERD

Mother Teresa and so many others have modeled their lifework after the example of Jesus. He was the most compassionate and loving leader who has ever lived. He called Himself the Good Shepherd: "I am the Good Shepherd; I know My own sheep, and they know Me" (John 10:14). *Good Shepherd* accurately describes the work that Jesus accomplished while He was on earth. Just what does this title mean?

If you live on a farm or in a rural area, you might know a thing or two about sheep. Maybe your kids or your neighbors down the road have raised a few to enter in 4-H competitions or the county fair. But if you're like most people in the United States, you don't encounter sheep very often. Perhaps you've only seen a real, live sheep at the petting zoo, and everything you know about shepherds you picked up from your church's annual Christmas pageant. Learning about the role of a shepherd and the characteristics of sheep can give us insight into what Jesus meant when He called Himself the Good Shepherd.

First, let's examine the nature of sheep. They aren't exactly heroic animals. Sheep have no defenses. Cats have claws; dogs have fangs; horses can gallop; goats have horns; but domestic sheep have none of these physical advantages. When sheep are under attack from a predator, they will stand rooted to the spot while other flock members are torn apart. At other times, sheep will run blindly when they are spooked by a noise that may be nonthreatening, like a rabbit running through the brush. Sheep are followers. They will amble off after another sheep down the same little trail, no matter how difficult the path or how lost they become.[3]

Does this description of sheep remind you of the human race? Because of our sin nature, we humans are ill equipped to defend ourselves against the attacks of a sinful world and the arrows of the devil. When we see others making destructive choices, we often fail to warn them of the danger. Instead of fleeing temptation, we stand rooted to the spot, putting ourselves in danger too. At other times, we get carried away by worries—dangers that exist only in our imaginations. We are followers—to our own detriment. People participate in risky behaviors even when they see how those habits destroy lives. How many times have you seen someone apply the "wisdom" of movie stars or other famous people to their own lives? Yet most movie stars live desperately corrupt lives.

Second, sheep need a shepherd to protect them and provide for their needs, someone who cares deeply for their welfare. A good shepherd takes his flock to green pastures and fresh water. He guards against predators and dangerous terrain. He knows each sheep by name, and they recognize his voice. At the end of the day he brings them back to the sheepfold, then watches all night so that no predator breaches the wall.

Jesus' heart ached for the people of His day. As He traveled throughout the Galilean countryside, teaching, preaching, and healing, "He felt great pity for the crowds that came, because their problems were so great and they didn't know where to go for help. They were like sheep without a shepherd" (Matthew 9:36). Jesus longed to comfort them and lead them along a safe path under His care and protection.

How does Jesus care for His human sheep? He leads them with compassion, wisely teaches them God's ways, prays for them, and protects them. Let's look at how Jesus fulfilled the role of Good Shepherd in these ways.

The Compassionate Shepherd

I once traveled from Orlando to Tallahassee, the Florida state capital, where I spoke to a distinguished body of people, including the governor and the chief justice of the state supreme court. I enjoyed the marvelous and moving two-hour program.

One of the highlights of the program was when an African-American woman told her story of how God had led her to adopt many children, most of whom were considered "unadoptable" because they were dying. She brought each of those hurting and forsaken children into her home and loved them. She taught them that they were children of God—that the girls were princesses and the boys were princes. She even went through a little ceremony where she took each child's hand and said, "I greet you, Prince Phillip." Or "I greet you, Princess Anne. You're a child of God." She communicated to those previously unloved children that they were deeply loved. Those children, who had known so many demeaning, damaging experiences, had their lives changed by someone who gave them unconditional love. I thought how well she displayed the same kind of love as the Jesus she served.

How did Jesus express His love? The Gospels are filled with examples of

His compassion. He healed every kind of disease—blindness, lameness, leprosy. When He healed the sick, He spoke to them gently, touched them, and gave them hope. Jesus also raised people from the dead. The most well-known story is that of Lazarus, who with his two sisters was a dear friend of Jesus. Jesus also miraculously fed the crowds who followed Him to hear Him teach. At one time, Jesus fed more than five thousand people with just five loaves of bread and two fish! The disciples had suggested sending the people away to fend for themselves, but Jesus saw the children, the old, the sick, the poor, and He met their needs.

Jesus became friends with the outcasts of society. The story of Zacchaeus is especially moving. He was a Jew who collected taxes for the Roman government. In those days, tax collecting was a corrupt line of work. The tax man squeezed as much as he could from each taxpayer, sent what was required to the government, and pocketed the rest. The other Jewish people hated tax collectors—with good reason.

One day Jesus was walking through the city of Jericho, followed by a large crowd. Zacchaeus was too short to see over the heads of the people in front of him, so he ran ahead and situated himself in the branches of a sycamore tree. The crowds came closer to Zacchaeus's perch. When Jesus came to the tree, He stopped, looked up into the branches, and said, "Zacchaeus! . . . Quick, come down! For I must be a guest in your home today" (Luke 19:5).

A murmur went through the crowd. They all knew Zacchaeus and what a swindler he was. Why would Jesus associate with the likes of him?

While the crowd saw Zacchaeus as a notorious sinner, Jesus saw one of His children in need of love and compassion. Zacchaeus was astounded. To be singled out by Jesus—He even knew his name! Immediately, Zacchaeus responded to the love Jesus showed him. He scrambled down the tree trunk, joy filling his face. He said, "I will give half my wealth to the poor, Lord, and if I have overcharged people on their taxes, I will give them back four times as much!" (Luke 19:8).

Like the woman who took in the unadoptable, dying children, Jesus let His compassion overrule the majority opinion. He made the previously unloved tax collector feel like a prince by showing him unconditional love. As a result, Zacchaeus's life was totally turned around!

The Wise Shepherd
Turning from sin to righteousness was one of the main themes of Jesus' teaching and stories. A good shepherd leads his flock down pathways to

green pastures and fresh water, away from briar patches, steep cliffs, and the hunting grounds of predators. In the same way, Jesus' teaching led His listeners down the right pathway of living to joy and goodness.

One of Jesus' most famous teachings is the Sermon on the Mount (see Matthew 5–7). In this sermon, He gave us the Beatitudes—principles about what God's Kingdom is like. His wisdom turned the prevailing "knowledge" of the day upside down. He elevated the poor, the gentle and lowly, the merciful, the pure, and the persecuted. Jesus spoke of God's standards concerning anger, adultery, revenge, love for enemies, love of money, and prayer. He gave us the Golden Rule: "Do for others what you would like them to do for you" (Matthew 7:12). His teaching amazed the crowds because His wisdom came from God and not the burdensome traditions of religion. Some of His lessons He gave to the masses, but other principles He reserved for those who were closest to Him and who would obey His teaching and pass it on to others. Still other times He spoke to individuals who came to Him seeking answers. Jesus always adjusted His teaching to the listener and the listener's heart, but He stayed true to the message God the Father had given Him.

Not long before He was arrested, Jesus gave what we call the Great Commandment. It is a summation of all He taught and all that God expects us to do. We find the Great Commandment in Matthew 22:37-40: "'You must love the Lord your God with all your heart, all your soul, and all your mind.' This is the first and greatest commandment. A second is equally important: 'Love your neighbor as yourself.' All the other commandments and all the demands of the prophets are based on these two commandments."

These two principles are the foundation of the teaching of Jesus. When we obey them, our lives will be full and satisfying.

The Praying Shepherd

Did you know that Jesus prayed for you while He was on earth? His most heartfelt prayer is found in John 17. The circumstances surrounding this prayer are especially poignant. He was in the garden of Gethsemane on the Mount of Olives. The disciples were with him, but they had all fallen asleep. Jesus was alone, facing what He knew would be an excruciating death. Within hours He would be arrested.

What did He pray? He put His life in the Father's hands, and then He prayed for His followers—including those in the future. "My prayer is not for the world, but for those you have given Me, because they belong to You. . . . I am praying not only for these disciples but also for all who will ever believe in Me because of their testimony" (John 17:9, 20). At the darkest hour of His life, Jesus wasn't consumed with His own feelings and needs, but He agonized in prayer over those who would serve and follow Him. As the Good Shepherd, He put the concerns of His sheep before His own safety. In the next chapter, we will find out just how much He was willing to give up for His sheep!

The Protective Shepherd

One of the most dangerous jobs a shepherd has is protecting his sheep. Phillip Keller, once a shepherd himself, tells the story of one boy who lived in East Africa. He was a member of the Masai people who raised sheep. Keller writes:

> Just a few days after we moved into the Masai country, a small, slim boy about ten years old was carried up to our house. He had, singlehanded, tackled a young lioness that tried to kill one of his flock. In total self-abandonment and utter bravery, he had managed to spear the lion. The mauling he took almost cost him his life. We rushed him to the nearest hospital twenty-seven miles away where his young life was spared, as by a thread. But why did he do this? Because the sheep were his. His love and honor and loyalty were at stake. He would not spare himself.[4]

How does Jesus protect His sheep? While He was on earth, He performed miracles. When His disciples were caught up in a fierce storm that threatened their boat, Jesus rebuked the wind and the waves—and they obeyed Him (see Mark 4:35-41). He healed Peter's mother-in-law, who was sick with a fever (see Mark 1:29-31). And like this Masai boy, Jesus took His responsibility for taking care of His sheep to the greatest degree.

One of the duties of a shepherd is to guard the sheepfold. He stands at the gate so that strangers cannot get in. Jesus says, "I assure you, I am the gate for the sheep, . . . All others who came before Me were thieves and robbers. But the true sheep did not listen to them. . . . Those who come in through Me will be saved. Wherever they go, they will find green pastures. The thief's purpose is to steal and kill and destroy. My purpose is to give life in all its fullness" (John 10:7-10). In these verses, Jesus is speaking of

His role in protecting the sheep from Satan and his evil forces. The Bible describes Satan as a roaring lion: "Be careful! Watch out for attacks from the Devil, your great enemy. He prowls around like a roaring lion, looking for some victim to devour" (1 Peter 5:8). The Good Shepherd has defeated our enemy, and we look to Him for protection from evil.

Another responsibility that a shepherd assumes is that of finding lost sheep. The shepherd knows each animal by name and misses any that wander from the flock. Have you ever seen a painting of Jesus as the Good Shepherd holding a trembling lamb in His arms? That is a beautiful representation of Him finding a straying lamb and bringing it back into the fold. Jesus says, "If a shepherd has one hundred sheep, and one wanders away and is lost, what will he do? Won't he leave the ninety-nine others and go out into the hills to search for the lost one? And if he finds it, he will surely rejoice over it more than over the ninety-nine that didn't wander away! In the same way, it is not My heavenly Father's will that even one of these little ones should perish" (Matthew 18:12-14).

Jesus takes His role of the Good Shepherd to the highest degree. He compassionately cares for those who belong to Him, leads them down the path to a full life, prays for their welfare, and protects them.

In John 10:11, Jesus makes a startling statement: "I am the Good Shepherd. The Good Shepherd lays down His life for the sheep." Jesus was willing to make the greatest sacrifice for us—giving up His life! What would make the Son of God take this humbling step? What did He accomplish through His death? These are the questions we will explore in the next chapter.

Truly, Jesus' lifework displayed the loving care of a good shepherd. You have the choice of living within His sheepfold or staying outside to face the forces of evil alone. Inside is safety and joy; outside is danger and despair. Have you placed your life in the hands of the Good Shepherd? If you have, do you completely trust Him with all you have and are? In the final two chapters of this section, we will discover just how fully we can trust in His care!

Discover Jesus

Read about the Real Jesus: Listen to what Jesus said about Himself as your Good Shepherd:

> I assure you, I am the gate for the sheep. . . . Yes, I am the gate. Those who come in through Me will be saved. Wherever they go, they will find green pastures. . . . I am the Good Shepherd. The Good Shepherd lays down His life for the sheep. . . . I am the Good Shepherd; I know My own sheep, and they know Me, just as My Father knows Me and I know the Father. And I lay down My life for the sheep.
>
> JOHN 10:7-15

1. Consider the problems in your life. How does it make you feel to know that Jesus sees and cares about your pain and sorrow?

2. What qualities about Jesus as the Good Shepherd are listed in the verses above?

3. What do these qualities mean to you?

4. How can you take your cares and worries to Jesus?

7

The Lamb of God

*I*magine what it must have been like for Jesus' friends during the horror of His arrest and trial. What were they feeling? They likely experienced a roller-coaster ride of emotions that ended in despair, fear, and utter disappointment. Let's take a firsthand look at that night through the eyes of John, one of Jesus' closest disciples.

John, "the disciple whom Jesus loved" (John 21:7), was with his Master and the rest of the disciples when they came into Jerusalem that Sunday before it all happened. Jesus was riding on a donkey, and a cheering crowd met them as they entered the city. The thunderous praise of all those people rang in John's ears: "Praise God for the Son of David! Bless the One who comes in the name of the Lord! Praise God in highest heaven!" (Matthew 21:9).

The people threw their coats and palm fronds in front of the donkey's feet, honoring Jesus. It seemed as if all Jerusalem was stirred. People appeared from all over the city, asking who this man was. The crowd answered, "It's Jesus, the prophet from Nazareth in Galilee" (Matthew 21:11).

John felt so proud. He was part of a rising movement that would change Jewish history! This was the moment when Jesus would take His rightful place as King of Israel. Gone would be the cruel Romans and the pompous Jewish religious leaders. John surely remembered the prophecy Zechariah had given hundreds of years before: "Look, your King is coming to you. He is righteous and victorious, yet He is humble, riding on a donkey—even on a donkey's colt" (Zechariah 9:9). That prophecy was being fulfilled right before John's eyes!

Despite the festive atmosphere, John was troubled by something Jesus had told His disciples—that He was going to die. John didn't understand how this could happen, so he pushed the thought away.

But as the events of that week unfolded, John could no longer ignore his troubling thoughts. On Thursday evening during the Passover meal, Jesus said that one of the disciples would betray Him. Afterward He took them to the garden of Gethsemane to pray. This was not unusual in itself, but then Jesus left eight of the disciples behind and took John, Peter, and James farther on. Jesus stopped and began to pray, His voice straining in anguish. Then He went on alone, leaving the three behind to continue praying. John felt so tired that he just couldn't keep his eyes open. Soon he and the other two disciples were sleeping soundly.

Suddenly John woke up to what seemed like a horrible nightmare! Soldiers marched up the path and confronted Jesus. A hostile mob was milling around the soldiers. Then Judas stepped out of the mob, walked up to Jesus, and kissed Him on the cheek. Immediately, the soldiers arrested Jesus and tied His hands. One of Jesus' own followers had betrayed Him to the religious leaders!

WHY DID THIS HAVE TO HAPPEN?

Why did Jesus have to come to earth? And why did He have to die? Couldn't God have accomplished His purposes another way? The answer goes back to God's nature. His unlimited qualities of love, mercy, justice, and holiness required a plan that would satisfy every part of His perfect nature. The problem was our sin.

Think of the world as a big courtroom. Let's go back to the beginning of time, when Adam and Eve were in the Garden of Eden. The world was perfect, just as God created it. Adam and Eve worked under God's hand, and their lives were joyful and fulfilling.

Then God's enemy, Satan, interfered in God's perfect world. God had given Adam and Eve access to everything in the Garden except one thing. He had told them not to eat from the tree of the knowledge of good and evil (see Genesis 2:15-17). He gave them the ability to choose between right and wrong. Satan saw his opportunity. He told Adam and Eve that if they ate from the tree, they would become like God (see Genesis 3:1-5). Adam and Eve obeyed Satan rather than God, and in doing so, they transferred their allegiance from God's kingdom to Satan's. Satan could say to God, "Aha! You see that I have taken over their hearts and minds. Their inclination is to sin, not to live holy lives!"

From then on, the human race has been consumed by sin. It is a universal problem. The Bible says, "All have sinned; all fall short of God's glorious standard" (Romans 3:23). Simply put, sin is anything that is contrary to what God commands or forbids in the Bible. John provides a clear definition: "Every wrong is sin" (1 John 5:17).

The root cause of sin is the deceitfulness and selfishness of the human heart. Have you ever thought, *I know this is wrong, but . . .* Or have you ever excused yourself with, "What I did wasn't that bad!" You are displaying an attitude common to the human race—the self-deception of a sinful heart. The prophet Jeremiah was aware of the heart's power to deceive. He writes, "The human heart is most deceitful and desperately wicked. Who really knows how bad it is?" (Jeremiah 17:9). Each of us is born with this natural tendency to sin. What a sobering thought that my own heart is more capable of deceiving me than any other evil and cunning power!

Perhaps you have been faced with a temptation that could get you into great trouble. A lie on your taxes. A flirtation with a married person. Stealing on the job. Peeking at a porn site on the Internet. Yet you did what many people do. You rationalized your actions. You convinced yourself that the danger was minimal and that you would come through unscathed. But somehow or somewhere in your life, you will pay the price for your bad decision.

Let's go back to the world's courtroom. God is sitting in the judge's seat, and you are standing in the place reserved for the guilty. Satan is your accuser. If he can prove that you have violated even one of God's rules, you will be condemned, for this is God's standard: "The wages of sin is death" (Romans 6:23).

Satan, of course, knows the verdict. God's kingdom is pure, holy, and perfect. No one who sins even one time belongs in His heavenly realm. Satan grins maniacally. Your fate is a foregone conclusion—guilty! The gavel pounds, and you are shut out of God's presence forever.

THE CONSEQUENCES OF SIN

Just as Satan is sure about the guilty verdict, he knows everything your sentence will involve. The Bible is clear about the consequences of sin.

Sin causes eternal death. Just as people earn a day's wages for working one day, sin results in a just payment. The prophet Ezekiel writes, "The one who sins is the one who dies" (18:20). We all must pay for what we have done. We can't pass on the debt to our parents or children; they will face God for their own sins. Many people believe that their sin will never be found out, but God sees everything.

Sin kills fellowship with God. When Adam and Eve gave in to temptation, God sent them out of the Garden. That's a picture of how our sin separates us from God—both here in this life and later for eternity. Our sin creates a wall between God and us.

Sin reaps physical death. One thing we all share is death. Because Adam sinned and thereby passed a sin nature on to all his descendants, all humanity is infected with the sin disease. The punishment for this disease is physical death.

Sin results in a final judgment. God has reserved a day of final judgment for every person ever born. We will have to stand before His throne and answer for every sin we have committed in our lifetime. As punishment, we will be banished from God's presence forever.

Right now you may be thinking, *I don't know all God's standards. How can He judge me on laws I've never heard?* Because they are written in our hearts as our conscience (see Romans 2:14-15). Through the following illustration, the great theologian Francis Schaeffer explains why we are all guilty.

Imagine that all babies are born with an invisible tape recorder hung around their necks. Imagine further that these are very special recorders that record only when moral judgments are made. Aesthetic judgments such as "This is beautiful" are not recorded. But whenever people make statements such as "She's a nosy gossip" or "He's so lazy," the machine records the statement. Many times each day the recorder operates as people make moral judgments about those around them, recording dozens of judgments each week, hundreds every year, and thousands in a lifetime.

Then the scene shifts, and we suddenly see all the people of the world standing before God at the end of time. "God, it's not fair for you to judge me," say some. "I didn't know about Christ. No one taught me the Ten Commandments, and I never read the Sermon on the Mount."

Then God speaks. "Very well. Since you claim not to know My laws, I will set aside My perfect standard of righteousness. Instead, I will judge you on this." As He pushes the button on the recorder that was with the person throughout his or her life, the person listens with growing horror to hear his or her own voice pour forth a stream of condemnation toward other people. Thousands upon thousands of condemning moral judgments play from the recorder.

When the tape ends, God says, "This is the basis of My judgment: how well you kept the moral standards you applied to those around you. You accused someone of lying, yet numerous times you stretched the truth. You were angry at that fellow for being selfish, yet on many occasions you put your own interests above someone else's needs."

In that day, every person will be silent. For no one will have consistently lived up to the standards he or she demanded of others.[1]

The impossibility of deserving God's acceptance is magnified when we realize that God does not require mere good works from us. He is morally perfect; thus He demands perfection. Jesus said, "You are to be perfect, even as your Father in heaven is perfect" (Matthew 5:48). That includes attitudes and actions. But who can be perfect? Moral perfection is so impossible that no one can attain it. This is why sin and its effects have been described as an infinite gap between God and sinners.

This is also why "religious" people—those who live outwardly good and moral lives but who do not know God in their hearts—can never reach God. Reaching God by doing good works is like trying to jump across the Grand Canyon. It is between six and eighteen miles across, 276 miles long, and one mile deep. The world's record in the long jump is less than 29 feet. A jumper could train for years and even break the world record, but he would still fall far short of the canyon wall on the other side. A two-year-old and a pro jumper would suffer the same fate—disaster!

Does this mean that the human plight is hopeless? Has Satan won? Oh, no! Before God created the world, He had a plan to remedy sin. And that plan centered on Jesus! God first revealed this plan in the Garden of Eden. Speaking to Satan, God said, "He [the Messiah] will crush your head, and you will strike His heel" (Genesis 3:15). We will see how accurate this prediction of the coming Messiah was.

JESUS TOOK OUR PUNISHMENT

During the era of Russian tribal history, a certain Russian leader had two laws. The first was that all people must love their parents, and the second was a prohibition against stealing. This man's leadership and these laws made his tribe superior in all of Russia.

One day someone broke the law against stealing, although the thief was not caught. This angered the leader, so he brought together all his people.

He demanded, "Let the thief come forward and receive ten lashes for his crime."

No one responded, so he increased the punishment to twenty lashes, then thirty, then forty. He stopped there because he knew that only a strong person could survive forty lashes.

The crowd dispersed, and the leader sent out his men to find the thief. A week later, they brought in the guilty person. The leader gasped. The thief was his own mother!

The guards began wagering among themselves. What would their leader do? Would he carry out his punishment for the second law of stealing and whip his mother? Or would he obey the first law of love and let his mother go free? If the crime went unpunished, every thief could argue that he or she should go free too.

The leader gathered the tribe together. The guards brought his mother forward, and the sentence was announced. They bared her frail back. *Aha, the people thought, he's going to whip her.*

Just before the whip master brought the lash across her back, the leader strode over. Taking off his own shirt, he took the forty lashes himself.

That's exactly the picture of what happens in God's courtroom. You are standing in judgment when God announces the sentence: eternal death. Satan is doing a victory dance, his face gleaming.

Then Jesus steps forward. "I will take the punishment in place of this person."

The grin is wiped off Satan's face. "But how can you do that?" he asks.

"Because I have never sinned. I became a human like this person. Therefore, I can take his place."

At that moment, the Good Shepherd exchanges His position as head of the flock for the most humble one, a lamb. As our substitute, the Bible calls Jesus the "Lamb of God who takes away the sin of the world" (John 1:29). What does this mean?

In the Old Testament system of worship, the high priest sacrificed a spotless lamb on the altar in the Temple once a year. The morning of Passover, the high priest led the lamb to the altar and tied it up. Then at three o'clock the high priest came back and killed the lamb. After he did this, he said, "It is finished." The lamb's blood was spilled to represent the fact that in God's judgment, death must occur for the payment of sin. The lamb pictured a future day when the Messiah's blood would be spilled on a cross to pay for the sins of the world. Jesus was that Lamb!

The Lamb of God conquered Satan and all evil. Jesus' death satisfied every part of God's perfect nature:

- His justice—Jesus paid the price for sin.
- His love—Jesus died in our place as a voluntary act of love.
- His mercy—Jesus' death pardons the condemned.
- His holiness—Jesus' death declares us free from sin, spotless.

Like the Russian tribal leader, Jesus stepped up and took the consequences for your sin and mine. The price of that gesture of love and justice is beyond our imagining. How I thank Him for that sacrifice.

THE BLOOD OF JESUS

But I was not always positive about Jesus' death on the cross. When I was a young man, the idea of the Cross offended me. My nature was affronted by talk of the blood of Jesus. Something about the Crucifixion account just seemed so reprehensible.

One day through an old hymn of the church, God revealed the meaning of the Cross to me, as only He can do:

> *What can wash away our sin?*
> *Nothing but the blood of Jesus.*
> *What can make us whole again?*
> *Nothing but the blood of Jesus.*
> *Oh, precious is the flow*
> *That makes me white as snow,*
> *No other fount I know,*
> *Nothing but the blood of Jesus.[2]*

Through those words, I saw that without the shed blood of Jesus, I could not have forgiveness of my sins. That was the meaning behind the title *Lamb of God*. Yes, the blood is offensive because my sin is so horrid. But when I realized what the blood of Jesus meant to me, it became precious!

This was a hard lesson for the disciples to learn as well. When the disciples ran away at Jesus' arrest, they did not understand that the plan was going just as God intended. Prophecy was being fulfilled in Jesus. But the disciples cowered and hid. Peter followed the soldiers from a distance and then denied he was Jesus' friend.

All night long, Jesus was dragged from one courtroom to another. He was beaten with whips until His back was raw. People spit on Him, called Him names, and shoved a crown of thorns on His head. They dressed Him in a purple robe and ridiculed Him. The people screamed for His crucifixion. What had happened to the adoring crowd of the Sunday before? Why was there so much hatred now?

The sentence was passed—crucifixion! Jesus was not condemned for crimes He committed. Even the Roman governor Pilate, who sentenced Him to death, admitted that Jesus was innocent. Jesus died because He claimed to be equal with God.

Early Friday morning the guards led Jesus out of Pilate's courtroom to a hill north of Jerusalem called Skull Hill. Some of the women who were His friends followed at a distance—and so did John. They were helpless to assist Him.

The soldiers nailed Jesus' hands and feet to the wooden cross and set the cross upright in a hole. John witnessed every horrible moment. How his heart must have ached! The guards posted a sign over Jesus' head—"Jesus of Nazareth, the King of the Jews." Then Jesus suffered slowly and excruciatingly for hours while the watching mob ridiculed Him.

At noon, alarming events began to happen. Darkness fell across the land for three hours, blotting out the sun. Finally Jesus cried out in His agony, "My God, My God, why have You forsaken Me?" (Matthew 27:46). God the Father had turned His back on His Son because Jesus had taken on His shoulders the sin of the world. God could not look upon sin, so He could not look upon His Son in His most desperate hour.

Then Jesus cried out, "It is finished!" and He gave up His spirit (John 19:30).

This was the exact moment when the high priest was sacrificing a lamb on the altar in the Temple for the sins of the people! If the priest would have looked, he could have seen God's real sacrificial Lamb, Jesus Christ![3] As soon as Jesus died, the thick curtain in the Temple that hid the Most Holy Place split in two. An earthquake shook the area. The Roman soldiers were so terrified that they shouted, "Truly, this was the Son of God!" (Matthew 27:54).

Jesus had paid the price—willingly and out of love for us. His body was taken down, prepared for burial, and put in a borrowed tomb before the holy Sabbath day began at nightfall. Because the religious leaders were afraid that someone would steal the body, Pilate ordered a huge stone rolled over the entrance, a seal placed over the stone, and guards around the tomb. No one could disturb the body of Jesus.

John must have thought that this was the end of the disciples' hopes and dreams. He had seen miracles, heard the Master's wisdom, felt the compassion of Jesus. But now it was Friday night and the holy day of Sabbath was about to begin. The Messiah had been murdered like a common criminal. Was God powerless? Was this the end of the prophecies?

Not quite. The story wasn't over by far. The greatest miracle was just hours away!

Read about the Real Jesus: What was the difference between Adam and Jesus?

> Adam's one sin brought condemnation upon everyone, but Christ's one act of righteousness makes all people right in God's sight and gives them life. Because one person disobeyed God, many people became sinners. But because one other person obeyed God, many people will be made right in God's sight.
>
> ROMANS 5:18-19

1. What is God saying about the choices people make and about how those choices affect their future?

2. What consequences do your sins have on others? How does that make you feel?

3. What actions and attitudes in your life do you think displease God?

4. How difficult is it for you to change these areas and attitudes? Could you ever completely free yourself from all your sin?

5. How does it make you feel to know that God loves you so much that He was willing to make the ultimate sacrifice for you—the life of His only Son?

8

The Miracle That Changed the World

*T*he greatest miracle the world has ever known was discovered by a most unlikely person. The miracle was the resurrection of our Lord Jesus Christ on the third day after He was crucified. The first person to see Him was Mary Magdalene, a woman whom everyone had once despised because of her immoral life.

Mary Magdalene and several other women who were followers of Jesus got up early on Sunday morning to go to the tomb where Jesus' body had been placed. They brought burial spices to anoint His body because the burial had been done so quickly on Friday evening that no one had prepared the body properly. As they walked, the women discussed how they were going to roll away the stone in front of the tomb. And how would they get past the Roman guards?

It was still dark when they arrived at the tomb, so it may have taken a minute before the women realized that the stone had been rolled away. Not only that, they discovered that the tomb was empty! Mary thought, *Someone has stolen the body of my Lord.*

The calamities never seemed to end. The despair of the moment must have been as dark as that early morning. Jesus had been the One who had accepted Mary when everyone else had shunned her. He had spoken to her so gently and forgiven her sins. He had included her in the warm company of those who surrounded Him. How she must have longed for His presence!

With sadness in her heart, she went back and told Peter and John that someone had stolen the Lord's body. The three of them ran back to the tomb to check it out. It was just as Mary had described. Peter ducked into the stone cavity and found the cloths that had been wrapped around the body. The face cloth was folded up beside the rest. John followed Peter into the tomb, and he saw it all too.

Think of how the sight of those burial wrappings must have seemed to Jesus' friends. If someone stole a body that had lain in a tomb for several days, why would they unwrap it and neatly fold up the face cloth? It made no sense. Peter and John turned around and went home.

But Mary didn't leave. She sobbed silently outside the tomb. Then she glanced inside. Someone was there! Two white-robed angels sat on the ledge where the body had lain. "Why are you crying?" they asked her.

"'Because they have taken away my Lord,' she replied, 'and I don't know where they have put Him'" (John 20:13).

Then she felt someone's presence behind her. She turned around and saw a man she supposed was the gardener. But it wasn't! It was Jesus! He was alive! He had risen from the dead. This was more than she had ever dreamed could happen.

How like Jesus to first appear to one who loved Him so much because of all He had done for her. He didn't choose the most esteemed of His followers or the most beautiful. He chose the woman who had needed Him so desperately.

WHY WAS THE RESURRECTION NECESSARY?

Do you comprehend the true meaning of the Easter story? It's not about chocolate rabbits and Easter egg hunts. It commemorates the day that Jesus rose victoriously from the dead, the moment that He conquered sin, death, and the grave. The Resurrection is the culmination of the greatest love and power the world has ever seen.

Many years ago when I was a student in seminary, I had the privilege of studying under the eminent Bible scholar Wilbur M. Smith. In his classic work *Therefore, Stand,* he explains the importance of the Resurrection: "If Christ can be said to have conquered death, then His own body must have been delivered from death's power. In no other way can we account for the empty tomb, and the appearance of Christ after His resurrection, and in no other way can we say that Christ conquered death, unless His body was raised on Easter day."[1]

In other words, to prove His divinity, Jesus showed that He has power over death. He had raised people from the dead during His ministry, but it's a whole other matter to raise one's self from the grave! Humanly speaking, that's impossible.

The Bible tells us, "If there is no resurrection of the dead, then Christ has not been raised. And if Christ has not been raised, then your faith is useless, and you are still under condemnation for your sins. . . . But the fact is that Christ has been raised from the dead" (1 Corinthians 15:16-17, 20). Any argument for the truth of Christianity stands or falls on our Lord's resurrection. It is not a fable; it is a historical fact.

THE BURIED SEED

The picture of Jesus' death and resurrection is that of a seed buried in the soil. What happens to the seed? It sprouts. New life begins.

According to a Persian legend, when God created the earth, it was barren and without any sign of life. In due time, God sent out an angel to scatter all sorts of seeds over the face of the earth. When Satan saw the seeds, he resolved to destroy God's work. He sent out his helpers to bury the seeds so that they would rot. But soon the seeds, nestled in the good soil, began to germinate and push their shoots above the ground. What Satan did not realize was that seeds have to be buried to produce living plants. And so the entire earth became a beautiful garden of flowers, grain, and blossoming trees.

That's similar to the plan Satan devised to destroy the human race. He figured that if he could kill Jesus, the sent One from God, God's plan would be ruined. So when the Messiah came, Christ's enemies, who were in league with Satan, killed our Lord and put Him in a tomb. They set a stone at the mouth of the tomb, supposing that force could keep the Son of God in the grave. They posted guards to make sure no one could steal the body and claim that Jesus had come back to life. They were so sure that Christ's body would remain in the tomb and rot.

But Satan and his cohorts were unknowingly completing God's purpose. What they did not realize was that like a seed, Jesus had to die and be buried to rise again. Just as a seed brings forth new life, Jesus brought forth life. He rose again, not only to prove that He is God in the flesh but also to give us a better life now and eternal life later. This is the true meaning of Easter.

EVIDENCE FOR THE RESURRECTION

After Mary had seen Jesus alive, she reported the miracle to the disciples. But they didn't believe her. One of the disciples was so adamant that Jesus was not alive that today he is called "doubting Thomas." Even when the living Christ stood before him, Thomas found it difficult to believe that this person truly was the Lord.

With great compassion, Jesus said to Thomas, "Put your finger here and see My hands. Put your hand into the wound in My side. Don't be faithless any longer. Believe!" (John 20:27).

Thomas felt the nail holes in Jesus' hands and the gash in His side where the soldier had pierced Him with a spear. Thomas exclaimed, "My Lord and my God!" (John 20:28). Thomas had changed his mind!

Like Thomas, I, too, found it incredible that a man could be crucified and three days later walk among the living. More than fifty years ago, I set out to prove whether or not the Resurrection is true. At that time I was not a believer but a skeptic in search of verifiable proof that the Easter story was real. Let me give you some of the evidence for the Resurrection that had a profound impact on me.

1. Old Testament prophecies of the Resurrection were fulfilled in Jesus. The resurrection of the One sent from God was foretold hundreds of years before the event. Then Jesus fulfilled the prophecies exactly. One of the prophecies was given by King David: "No wonder My heart is filled with joy, and My mouth shouts His praises! My body rests in safety. For You will not leave My soul among the dead or allow Your godly One to rot in the grave" (Psalm 16:9-10).

After the Resurrection on the Day of Pentecost, Peter quotes that very prophecy in his sermon, then adds:

> Dear brothers, think about this! David wasn't referring to himself when he spoke these words I have quoted, for he died and was buried, and his tomb is still here among us. But he was a prophet, and he knew God had promised with an oath that one of David's own descendants would sit on David's throne as the Messiah. David was looking into the future and predicting the Messiah's resurrection. He was saying that the Messiah would not be left among the dead and

that His body would not rot in the grave. This prophecy was speaking of Jesus, whom God raised from the dead, and we all are witnesses of this. (Acts 2:29-32)

2. The Resurrection is the only reasonable explanation for the empty tomb. Although some people claimed that Jesus had not been killed but only weakened by the Crucifixion, if that had been the case, the stone in front of the sepulcher and the soldiers guarding the entrance would have prevented His escape. If Jesus' friends had tried to steal His body, the stone and the guards would have stopped them. Jesus' enemies had no motive to steal the body themselves since that would have only encouraged belief in Jesus as God. The only answer for the empty tomb that makes sense is that Jesus was no longer dead.

3. Jesus appeared to many witnesses after the Resurrection. The Bible records that more than five hundred people saw Jesus in person after His resurrection. These included the women at the tomb, the eleven disciples, a crowd of more than five hundred on a Galilean mountain, and the apostle Paul (see 1 Corinthians 15:5-8).

4. The beginning of the church proves the Resurrection. More than half of the first sermon recorded in Acts declared the truth of the Resurrection. We read a portion earlier, where Peter claimed to have seen Jesus alive. Philip Schaff, a highly esteemed church historian, describes how important the Resurrection was to the early church: "The Christian church rests on the resurrection of its Founder. Without this fact, the church could never have been born; it would soon have died a natural death. The miracle of the resurrection and the existence of Christianity are so closely connected that they must stand or fall together."[2]

Without the Resurrection and the witnesses to the event, the church would have failed in the first few centuries.

5. After the Resurrection, the lives of Jesus' followers were miraculously transformed. Every one of Jesus' disciples deserted Him during His trial and crucifixion. While He was in the grave, they huddled behind locked doors. Yet after the Resurrection, these same men and women were so convinced that Jesus was alive that they withstood persecution and martyrdom to tell the message of Jesus Christ. Would these people have given their lives for the cause of Christ if they had believed that the Resurrection was a fable? Surely not!

6. Jesus Christ is still transforming millions of lives worldwide. Through the work of our worldwide mission organization, I have seen the miracle of new spiritual life reproduced over and over on all continents of the globe. Men, women, and children are placing their trust in the risen Lord—and their lives are transformed. These are a few examples:

- Lubov, an atheistic teacher, received Christ as her Savior in Vladimir, Russia. Two and a half months later, she was teaching her eighth-grade class about the life of Jesus.

- A Christian in Winnipeg, Canada, knocked on the door of a family who lived a block from his church. He gave the family a video on the life of Jesus. They watched it, and the whole family wanted to know Christ. They passed the video on to another family. In all, thirteen people in three families made a decision to follow Jesus.

- In Borneo an eighty-year-old woman approached an American Christian who was helping the people in the area. Forty years ago, a missionary had come through and told the villagers about Jesus. The woman had heard about Jesus then but had not understood how to receive Him as her Savior. She had waited her entire life, and finally she heard the Good News. She was overjoyed.[3]

- In California a family of four was breaking up because the wife was having an affair. A Christian at the husband's workplace reached out to help, and the entire family heard about Jesus. Today the family has repaired the damage, and all are serving Christ and growing in their faith.

A transformed, new life can be yours too. But only one person can accomplish it—Jesus Christ!

THE TIME IS NOW

Many years ago I had the pleasure of visiting the ancient city of Jerusalem, where I sat inside the tomb in which Bible scholars believe Jesus was buried. I went to this garden with great excitement. Somehow I felt that my wonderful Lord would meet me there in a unique and special way as He had done in no other place and at no other time in my life.

Silently, I waited alone. Time passed, and nothing happened. I was disappointed. Then I remembered the words of those angels who spoke to Mary on that miraculous Sunday: "Why are you looking in a tomb for someone who is alive? He isn't here! He has risen from the dead!" (Luke 24:5-6).

At that moment I understood as I never had before that the Lord Jesus, the risen Christ, was with me in that tomb just as He was with me in every other place. As the risen Christ, He is present everywhere through His Spirit. I don't need to go to a special place to meet Him. He is always with me.

Today the real meaning of Easter can become a real part of your life—more than just a story. When you receive the risen Lord into your heart by faith, you will discover what millions have come to know—the life-giving power that only Jesus offers. The One who rose from the dead in victory over sin, death, and Satan will come into your life and transform you into a new person. That doesn't mean that you will never suffer loss, feel pain, or struggle with the turmoil of life. Rather, in the midst of it all, you will know a supernatural peace, love, and joy that will transcend every grief and every challenge life throws your way. And you will experience the freedom of a forgiven life!

No matter who you are—young or old, a professional or a student, married or single—at this very moment, you can make the decision of your lifetime. You have met the real Jesus and discovered what He has done for you out of His great love. He offers you the same wonderful love and plan that hundreds of millions through the centuries have received. He has already paid the penalty for your sin. He is asking you, in the quietness of your heart, to yield your all to Him—your intellect, will, and emotions. God has given us this promise: "For God so loved the world that He gave His only Son, so that everyone who believes in Him will not perish but have eternal life" (John 3:16). This truth is given for you. But you must make the decision to receive Christ as your Savior and Lord. In the world courtroom where God is judge, when Jesus steps forward to take your punishment, you must agree to the transaction. When you do, God promises, "To all who believed Him and accepted Him, He gave the right to become children of God" (John 1:12).

This step is taken by faith, not by any good deeds you can do. Paul explains: "God saved you by His special favor when you believed. And you can't take credit for this; it is a gift from God. Salvation is not a reward for the good things we have done, so none of us can boast about it" (Ephesians 2:8-9).

Receiving Christ involves turning to God from self by repenting of your sins and trusting Jesus to come into your life to forgive your sins and make you into the person He wants you to be. Just agreeing intellectually that Jesus is the Son of God and that He died and rose again is not enough. We each receive Him by faith, as an act of our will.

You can receive Jesus right now by faith through prayer. God knows your heart and is not as concerned with the words you say as He is with the attitude of your heart. Here is a prayer that has helped many people express faith in Jesus and invite Him into their lives:

Lord Jesus, I want to know You personally. Thank You for dying on the cross for my sins. I open the door of my life and receive You as my Savior and Lord. Thank You for forgiving my sins and giving me eternal life. Take control of my life and make me the kind of person You want me to be. Amen.

If you prayed this prayer sincerely from your heart, you have just received the Lord Jesus Christ as your personal Savior and Lord. You are now a child of God. You have begun a relationship with the God of the universe. Your life will never be the same!

YOUR FIRST LOVE

Perhaps you made the decision to receive Christ some time ago but your excitement for Him has dimmed. Or maybe you started out well in your Christian life but have had few opportunities to grow in your faith. Jesus was concerned about His followers who had lost their first love for Him. He says, "I know all the things you do. I have seen your hard work and your patient endurance. . . . But I have this complaint against you. You don't love Me or each other as you did at first! Look how far you have fallen from your first love!" (Revelation 2:2-5).

God makes His wonderful, boundless love available to us every moment of every day. How could we live without it? How could our first love for Him ever slip away when His love is so perfect and faithful? And yet I realize that it is a genuine danger for every Christian.

Can you point to a time in your life when your heart was on fire for Jesus? Did you love Christ with such a passion that people noticed? Did they see the transformation happening in your life?

For many reasons and without intending it, we let the flames die down until they become glowing embers. Soon only a wisp of smoke and ashes remain of our excitement for Jesus. Few things are sadder than the ashes of a burned-out devotion.

But there is good news! You can set your heart right again—back to your former love for Jesus. *Come home*—that is the message of Jesus. In simplest terms, the path back to our first love as given in Revelation 2:5 is this:[4]

What We Do	What We Use	What Christ Calls It
We think.	Mind	"Look how far . . ."
We feel.	Heart	". . . you have fallen from your first love!"
We change.	Soul	"Turn back to me again . . ."
We work.	Strength	". . . and work as you did at first."

God's plan uses our mind, heart, soul, and strength—everything about us—to bring us back into His presence. He wants *all* of us so that we may experience all of *Him*. I urge you, whatever your situation, to place yourself in the loving hands of the Good Shepherd. He is the only One we can trust with our lives and our eternal future. Do this in prayer, telling God you are sorry for your apathy toward Him and asking Him to help you restore your first love for Jesus.

As you take this step, you will find that your heart is ready to respond to His love. Just as a bride responds to her new husband's affection, you will experience a fresh and invigorating new way to live and work. The love of God will flow through you and spread to other people in all you do.

In the next section, we will learn how to respond to God's great love for us. He has provided examples through His Son of how we can channel the overflow of His love to others. As we do, we will experience joy and adventure in our lives!

Discover Jesus

Read about the Real Jesus: What did God do for you through Jesus Christ?

> God is so rich in mercy, and He loved us so very much, that even while we were dead because of our sins, He gave us life when He raised Christ from the dead. (It is only by God's special favor that you have been saved!)
>
> EPHESIANS 2:4-5

1. How does it make you feel when you realize that God loves you so much that He extended mercy to you because of Jesus?

2. If you have received the risen Jesus Christ into your heart by faith, how has He transformed your life?

3. If you haven't received Christ, what is keeping you from responding to God's love with all your heart, mind, soul, and strength?

4. Is it easy or difficult for you to believe in the truth of Jesus' resurrection? Why?

5. How does Christ's victory over death and the grave change your feelings about death and dying?

6. Thank God right now for all that He has given you through His Son, Jesus.

PART 3

How Do I Respond to Jesus?
~

I am the vine; you are the branches. Those who remain in Me, and I in them, will produce much fruit. For apart from Me you can do nothing.

JESUS

9

Christic in Me

$\mathcal{D}$avid faced a major decision in his life, one that would require him to sacrifice his dreams. He was a junior at the University of California, Davis, and had phenomenal talent as a kicker on the college football team. But his dilemma was that his brother Tommy had developed kidney failure. Members of the family were being tested to see if they would match as a living kidney donor. After a lot of prayer, David agreed to be tested too.

The tests showed that David was the closest match. If he chose to donate his kidney, he knew that his football career was over—he could not play with only one kidney. But he decided that his brother's life was more important to him than his football career, so he agreed to donate his kidney. After a successful operation, Tommy's health was restored.[1]

Where did David find the strength to make a decision that changed his whole future?

Karen had quite a different problem. She taught a fifth-grade class in a public school. One day a student asked her in class, "Are you afraid to die?"

Immediately, more questions popped up from other students about Jesus and heaven. Karen realized that the questions were coming up because Campus Crusade's *JESUS* Video Project ministry had mailed a video copy of the *JESUS* film to every home in the city. The children had watched the video about the life and death of Jesus, and now they had serious questions about what they had seen.

Karen began to pray silently. She knew that discussing religion in the classroom might cause her to lose her job. But her students were so eager to learn the answers to their questions, and most of them knew no one with whom they could discuss spiritual issues.

First, Karen allowed any student who felt uncomfortable with the topic to leave the room. No one moved. Then she talked to the students about who Jesus is and what He has done for us. She led the class in prayer, helping many to receive Jesus as their Savior.

Her thirty students were so enthused about Jesus that they led thirty more students to Him without any adult help. Karen told her principal what she had done, and although he was not excited about her actions, he agreed to support her because the students had brought up the discussion. Later at a graduation ceremony where the fifth-grade students were promoted to the nearby middle school, she presented each of the sixty new believers with a Bible that had their name embossed in gold.

Karen says, "I might still lose my job, but it would be worth it."[2]

Where did Karen find the courage to speak about Jesus in her classroom?

You may be facing a situation right now that seems to be more than you can handle:

- A persistent temptation that you just can't resist
- A crisis that seems so dark you feel the future is hopeless
- A relationship that is so contentious you can barely tolerate it
- A sense of guilt that is eating you up inside
- A family situation that has destroyed the peace in your home

Life certainly has its peaks and its valleys. But often the valleys seem to last much longer than the peaks! Hard situations occur much more frequently than joyful ones.

Perhaps you are thinking right now, *I wish Jesus were here to tell me what to do. I wish I could take a walk with Him and talk through my problem.* Even though Jesus is not present in the flesh to tell you what to do and to encourage you, He is with you. The Bible tells us that right now Jesus is sitting in heaven next to God the Father and that He has provided everything you need to live a supernatural life. In fact, as we will find out, we have access to God's presence in ways the disciples who walked and talked with Jesus in the flesh did not.

But our adventure in Christian living all depends on how we respond to Jesus. That is what this section of the book is about—learning how to live in joy and abundance. In this chapter, I will share with you the answer to several questions that will put you on the glorious pathway to the abundant life:

- Why did Jesus leave the earth after His resurrection?
- What did Jesus promise us about His Spirit?
- How can I experience consistent victory in my Christian life through the power of Jesus Christ?

Once we learn the basics of living with Jesus' Spirit, we will have what is necessary to experience other areas of Christian living.

THE PROMISE

Before His death, Jesus was concerned for His followers. When the disciples were with Him in the upper room where they all shared the Last Supper, Jesus began giving them instructions on what was going to happen in the near future. He told them that He was going to heaven to be with His Father.

Peter, who usually spoke up first, protested that he wanted to go with Jesus. Thomas was concerned that the disciples wouldn't know how to follow Him to the place where He was going.

The disciples were afraid of being left behind. They had spent three and a half years with the Master and had grown used to His leadership. They had left everything to follow Him. What would they do when He was gone?

But Jesus knew that His leaving was the best thing for His followers. How could that be? They wouldn't be able to see Him, touch Him, or learn from Him. But God had a plan that surpassed anything the disciples could imagine. This is the promise that Jesus gave His friends: "I will ask the Father, and He will give you another Counselor, who will never leave you. He is the Holy Spirit, who leads into all truth. The world at large cannot receive Him, because it isn't looking for Him and doesn't recognize Him. But you do, because He lives with you now and later will be in you. No, I will not abandon you as orphans—I will come to you" (John 14:16-18).

What was Jesus promising His disciples? That His Spirit would live in all believers. In other words, the moment a person receives Christ as Savior, the Holy Spirit sets up residence in his or her life.

Why was this such good news for the disciples? Because when Jesus lived with them, He could only be in one place at any one time. When He was in Nazareth, He couldn't be in Jerusalem. When He was sleeping, He couldn't be teaching. But the Holy Spirit does not have these limitations. He can be in all places at all times because He is the Spirit of God.

WHO IS THE HOLY SPIRIT?

The Holy Spirit is the third person of the triune God—Father, Son, and Holy Spirit. Although I could share many things about the Holy Spirit, the most important to us is that when we become children of God, Christ takes up residence in our hearts. He accomplishes this by sending the Holy Spirit. By faith, the very same Jesus about whom we are reading in this book enters your life in a new and exciting way to provide you the most glorious life imaginable. He gives you a new heart. He provides the power to break the grip of sin. In essence, you can think of the Holy Spirit as *Christ in you.* The apostle Paul explains, "This is the secret: Christ lives in you, and this is your assurance that you will share in His glory" (Colossians 1:27).

This is a hard concept to understand. Let me describe the interrelation-ship of the Trinity by comparing the three persons to an apple. An apple has three parts—the skin, the flesh, and the seeds. Each part is 100 percent apple. Yet each part also performs a unique function for the apple. The skin protects the flesh; the flesh provides nutrients for the seeds; and the seeds produce the new plant. Of course, this analogy is simplistic com-pared to the complexity and glory of God. But this is the principle: Each person in the Trinity is wholly and fully God. At the same time, each person carries out different responsibilities. Their actions are perfectly coordi-nated. Therefore, when the Bible says that the Holy Spirit resides in each believer's life and calls this fact "Christ living in you," all of that is true. The Father, Son, and Holy Spirit are one, so when you have one, you have all of God. The Holy Spirit is the Spirit of Christ living in you. The Holy Spirit will always represent what Christ taught and stood for. In fact, the Holy Spirit played an essential part in the ministry of Jesus.

THE POWER OF JESUS

When you look at the life of Jesus, where do you think He got the power to resist temptation and complete God's will? He accomplished so much in three and a half years!

- He healed many people of all kinds of diseases.
- He taught His disciples about God's Kingdom and trained them to teach others.
- He resisted the devil's temptations.
- He preached throughout the Galilean area.
- He raised people from the dead.
- He defended verbal attacks from the religious leaders.
- He helped sinners deal with their sin problems.
- He suffered and died on the cross.

My list could go on much longer, but you can see that Jesus packed those few short years full of ministry. Of course, He was God, but He also worked within a body of flesh and got tired and hungry. His feet got sore from walking, and His body grew weary from so many demands on His time. He suffered just like you and I do.

The Bible tells us that Jesus worked in the power of the Holy Spirit. Isaiah predicted that the coming Messiah would be filled with the Spirit:

Out of the stump of David's family will grow a shoot—yes, a new Branch bearing fruit from the old root. And the Spirit of the Lord will rest on Him—the Spirit of wisdom and understanding, the Spirit of counsel and might, the Spirit of knowledge and the fear of the Lord. He will delight in obeying the Lord. . . . He will defend the poor and the exploited. . . . He will be clothed with fairness and truth. (Isaiah 11:1-5)

In another Old Testament passage, God describes Jesus: "Look at My servant, whom I strengthen. He is My chosen one, and I am pleased with Him. I have put My Spirit upon Him" (Isaiah 42:1).

Matthew writes of Jesus' baptism at the beginning of His ministry: "As Jesus came up out of the water, the heavens were opened and He saw the Spirit of God descending like a dove and settling on Him. And a voice from heaven said, 'This is my beloved Son, and I am fully pleased with Him'" (Matthew 3:16-17). Do you see how perfectly that fulfills the prediction in Isaiah?

And Peter says: "No doubt you know that God anointed Jesus of Nazareth with the Holy Spirit and with power. Then Jesus went around doing good and healing all who were oppressed by the Devil, for God was with Him" (Acts 10:38).

Because the Trinity acts as one, Jesus never did anything without the Father's permission and without the power of the Holy Spirit. That is the example for us. If Jesus needed the power of the Spirit, how much more do we?

THE HOLY SPIRIT'S WORK

While all Christians become believers through the work of the Holy Spirit, that does not mean that all believers are *filled* and *controlled* by the Spirit. We choose what will control our lives. That's a decision of the will. Only when believers surrender their lives to Christ's control are they able to live in the Holy Spirit's power.

Let's explore this truth beginning with the fact that the Bible tells us that there are three kinds of people: the natural person, the spiritual person, and the worldly person. Looking at the diagrams of these three people will help us understand the importance of who's in control of our lives.

The Natural Person

The natural person is the person we are "by nature," without God. The Bible says, "People who aren't Christians can't understand these truths from God's Spirit. It all sounds foolish to them because only those who have the Spirit can understand what the Spirit means" (1 Corinthians 2:14). The diagram below illustrates the position of the natural person. The throne represents the control center of the life. Self (S) is on the throne, running the show. The cross, which represents Jesus, is outside this person's life. The circles represent situations in the natural person's life, and they are in chaos. This is the way we are by nature; we are alienated from God. The natural person is the self-directed person, not at all yielded to the Holy Spirit.

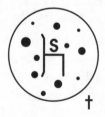

The Spiritual Person

The spiritual person is the person who has received Christ as Savior and has surrendered his or her life to Christ's control. "We who have the Spirit understand these things . . . for we have the mind of Christ" (1 Corinthians

2:15-16). With Christ on the throne, the spiritual person experiences all that God has because he or she lives in full submission to Christ. Self has relinquished control to the Holy Spirit. The Christ-directed person is empowered by the Holy Spirit. Notice in the next diagram that the situations in this person's life are orderly, not chaotic.

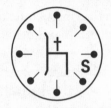

The Worldly Person

The worldly person is a believer, but the person has not surrendered fully to Christ's authority and control. As a result, this believer does not live in the power of the Holy Spirit. The apostle Paul says of this person, "Dear brothers and sisters, when I was with you I couldn't talk to you as I would to mature Christians. I had to talk as though you belonged to this world or as though you were infants in the Christian life. I had to feed you with milk and not with solid food, because you couldn't handle anything stronger. And you still aren't ready, for you are still controlled by your own sinful desires. You are jealous of one another and quarrel with each other. Doesn't that prove you are controlled by your own desires? You are acting like people who don't belong to the Lord" (1 Corinthians 3:1-3). The worldly person does not live victoriously because he or she is trying to live the Christian life in his or her own strength. In the final diagram, Christ is in this person's life, but He is not on the throne. Self remains in control, or self reclaims the control. Notice that the worldly person's life is in disorder.

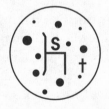

It's obvious from these diagrams that the person who is truly living a joyful, abundant life is the one who has chosen to place Christ on the throne. This person's life is directed and empowered by Christ's Spirit. How can we live this life?

SUPERNATURAL LIVING

Jesus gave His disciples an illustration that shows just how much we need to rely on the Holy Spirit's control. Jesus compared our lives to the branches of a grapevine: "I am the vine; you are the branches. Those who remain in Me, and I in them, will produce much fruit. For apart from Me you can do nothing" (John 15:5).

A branch never develops its own sap. Instead, the branch receives its sap and nutrients from the vine to which it is attached. As long as the branch is connected to the vine, the branch grows leaves and fruit. But the moment the branch is severed from the vine, it dries up.

This is a picture of the work of the Holy Spirit in our lives. Many Scripture passages tell us the benefits of living in the power of Christ's Spirit. Jesus said, "My purpose is to give life in all its fullness" (John 10:10). Paul writes, "When the Holy Spirit controls our lives, He will produce this kind of fruit in us: love, joy, peace, patience, kindness, goodness, faithfulness, gentleness, and self-control" (Galatians 5:22-23).

Are you experiencing the kind of life that Jesus offers? Do you find the fruit of the Spirit growing in you? Are you influencing people around you for Jesus? You can. I have seen this happen in my life and in the lives of so many other believers. As Scripture says, the secret is Christ living in you. When Christ is on the throne of our lives, the Holy Spirit gives us the power to live supernaturally.

Christ in Me

Christ's Spirit is our source of power. My friend Craig Lawrence discovered this as a successful businessman. He started and ran two TV stations and owned an advertising agency in his home state of South Dakota. Yet he felt a growing sense of discontentment. One day he traveled to a retreat center to talk to God. He told his wife, Marcia, "I'm not coming back until God speaks." At the retreat center, he dropped to his knees and cried tears over his seemingly wasted thirty-four years. He told God, "I'll do anything and give You everything." Craig gave Christ control of his life that day, and the Holy Spirit stepped in to give him the power to live a meaningful life for God.

I met Craig shortly after his decision to live under the control of the

Holy Spirit, when he agreed to serve as my communications director. His life completely changed and became an adventure in a way that his business success had never provided. In the 1990s Craig and Marcia felt God leading them to Mongolia, a country that had just been opened up to the gospel. The couple and their team were the largest delegation of Americans ever to visit the Communist nation at that time.

While they were in their hotel room, a detail of Mongolian soldiers came to take Craig and the team members to a government office building. When a group of Mongolian politicians asked the group who they were, Craig replied, "We are men whose hearts have been changed by Jesus Christ. When we asked Him where we should go to tell of His love, He sent us here."

At that moment, a Mongolian committee was drafting a new constitution for the Mongolian people. The committee was stuck on the topic of religious freedom—they didn't know how to write it into law. The leader asked the Christian team from the United States to help them write their constitution.

What an opportunity was laid before a businessman who had come from a relatively unpopulated state in the United States! Eventually the team not only helped write the constitution but also helped start a TV station in Mongolia, a task that fit Craig's past business experience so well. The new TV station carries many Christian programs, including testimonies from Mongolian Christians.[3] Craig will tell you that he is an ordinary man but that God has turned his life into an extraordinary journey through the power of the Spirit.

God calls each of us to serve Him in a unique way. Whatever He has designed for your life will fit your personality and will give you more joy and pleasure than any worldly attainment.

The only solution to the problems in the lives of both unbelievers and believers is repentance over sin and a desire to live a Spirit-filled life. But just what does it mean to be Spirit filled?

Being Filled with the Spirit

Being filled with the Holy Spirit means giving Jesus complete control of your life. In other words, the Spirit-filled life is the "Christ-directed" life in which Jesus lives through us in the power of the Holy Spirit.

This is how I practice living a Christ-directed life: I consider my body as a suit of clothes for Jesus, in which I have exchanged my former life of failures and defeat for His life of victory. This is the full (abundant) life mentioned in John 10:10. All of me—my body, mind, and spirit—is a vehicle for Christ to live His miraculous life through me. Paul expresses it this way, "I myself no longer live, but Christ lives in me" (Galatians 2:20).

If you ask for the filling of the Holy Spirit, God will fulfill His part because of His *command* and His *promise.* He has commanded us to be filled with the Spirit. Paul writes, "Don't be drunk with wine, because that will ruin your life. Instead, let the Holy Spirit fill and control you" (Ephesians 5:18).

God promises that He will always answer when we pray according to His will. John writes, "We can be confident that He will listen to us whenever we ask Him for anything in line with His will. And if we know He is listening when we make our requests, we can be sure that He will give us what we ask for" (1 John 5:14-15). Because God has *commanded* us to be filled with His Spirit, He will fulfill His *promise* to do so when we ask.

You can invite the Holy Spirit to completely fill your life right now. Read the following verses and take the steps.

- First, sincerely desire to be directed and empowered by the Spirit (see Matthew 5:6; John 7:37-39).
- Second, confess your sins, and by faith thank God that He has forgiven all your sins because of Christ (see Colossians 2:13-15; 1 John 2:1-3; Hebrews 10:1-17).
- Third, present every area of your life to God (see Romans 12:1-2).
- Fourth, by faith claim the fullness of the Holy Spirit (see Ephesians 5:18).

We are filled with the Spirit through faith. True prayer is one way of expressing your faith. The following is a prayer you can use to ask for the Holy Spirit's filling:

Dear Father, I need You. I acknowledge that I have been directing my own life, and that as a result, I have sinned against You. I thank You that You have forgiven my sins through Christ's death on the cross for me. I now invite Christ to again take His place on the throne of my life. Fill me with the Holy Spirit as You commanded me to be filled and as You promised in Your Word that You would do if I ask in faith. I now thank You for directing my life and for filling me with the Holy Spirit. Amen.

Does this prayer express the desire of your heart? If so, bow in prayer, and trust God to fill you with the Holy Spirit. Do not depend on your feelings. Because God promises to fill you, He will. God's promise—not our feelings—is our authority. As you step out in faith by the power of the Holy Spirit, your feelings will come along. And when we give the Holy Spirit control over our lives, we will be filled to overflowing with the holy presence of Jesus!

Spiritual Breathing

But what happens when we sin once again? As people with a human nature, we are bound to fail our Lord many times. The Holy Spirit cannot continue to fill us in the presence of obvious sin. When you retake control of the throne of your life through sin, you need to get rid of that sin and resurrender your life. You can do that through a process I call spiritual breathing.

What is spiritual breathing? Let me explain.

In the beginning of my Christian journey, God gave me a strong desire to live a holy life. I really worked at this matter of being a Christian. I attended church several times a week, led a group of more than a hundred young people who regularly told others about Jesus' love, and served as a deacon in my church. I studied and memorized Scripture and lived a disciplined life of prayer. Yet the harder I tried to live the Christian life, the more frustrated I became. I often felt guilty and spiritually inadequate.

One day as I was reading God's Word, He graciously showed me how a person can receive the fullness and power of the Holy Spirit to live a consistently godly and fruitful life. He revealed to me the concept I call *spiritual breathing*. For nearly fifty years I have experienced the exciting, wonderful, and adventurous joy of walking in the Spirit. This concept has also helped millions of Christians around the world experience God's love and forgiveness.

What happens when you breathe? You exhale the impure air and inhale the pure. When you exhale, your body rids itself of carbon dioxide and other impurities that would cause your body to become dysfunctional. Then when you inhale, you breathe in the oxygen that is crucial to maintaining a healthy body.

So it is with our spiritual lives. When we sin, our fellowship with God is broken. That is why we feel distant from God and become discouraged and complacent. But through spiritual breathing, we can enjoy renewed fellowship with God. Spiritual breathing is simply exhaling the impure (sin) and inhaling the pure (the power of the Holy Spirit). It is an exercise in faith. Here is how it works:

- *Exhale*—Confess your sin by agreeing with God concerning your sin, repenting of what you have done, and thanking God for His forgiveness (see 1 John 1:9; Hebrews 10:1-25). Repenting is changing your attitude and actions.
- *Inhale*—Surrender the control of your life to Christ and ask Him to fill you with His Holy Spirit. Trust that He now directs and empowers you according to the command in Ephesians 5:18 and the promise in 1 John 5:14-15.[4]

Continue to practice this process of spiritual breathing whenever you need to repent or when you have taken back control of your own life. If necessary, practice it many times a day. It will transform your life!

Once when my wife, Vonette, and I were in Washington, D.C., to attend a conference, a woman who was a leader of a Christian organization approached me. She said, "I have wanted to tell you this for years. I grew up in a Christian denomination where every time a person did anything wrong, he had to go to the altar and ask forgiveness. I was always at the altar, and I was living in defeat most of the time. Then I heard you speak on spiritual breathing, and I began to practice it. That was about twenty-five years ago, and my life has been transformed. All these years I have experienced the privilege of breathing spiritually."

Now that you are equipped with the supernatural power of the Holy Spirit to live a life above the ordinary, you can respond to Jesus in appropriate and pleasing ways. You can begin this new life that will take you places you never dreamed you could go.

What does God have in store for you? It may be to serve Him in a new way right where you are. Or it may be to volunteer to serve Him in another part of the world. You will be an influence for Jesus at your workplace or school. Certainly you can be Christ's witness in your family. Whatever God calls you to do, He gives you Christ's Spirit to enable you to accomplish it.

In our next chapter, we will see just what we are able to do in our Christian lives. Jesus has given us the instructions and the example. His Spirit gives us the power. Are you ready for all that God has prepared for you?

Discover Jesus

Read about the Real Jesus: Read the command and the promise that enable you to live a supernatural life:

> **Command:** Don't be drunk with wine, because that will ruin your life. Instead, let the Holy Spirit fill and control you.
>
> EPHESIANS 5:18

> **Promise:** We can be confident that He will listen to us whenever we ask Him for anything in line with His will. And if we know He is listening when we make our requests, we can be sure that He will give us what we ask for.
>
> 1 JOHN 5:14-15

1. In what areas of your life do you feel inadequate to live as Jesus wants you to live?

2. What sins have come between you and God, damaging your fellowship with Him?

3. How do you think your life will change if you practice spiritual breathing on a consistent basis?

4. What would you like to do for Jesus that you can't accomplish now?

5. How will being filled with the Holy Spirit help you serve God in this area?

10

The Love of Jesus

*T*wo words describe the heart of Nus Reimas: extraordinary love. He grew up in the paradise of the Indonesian province of Maluku. He and his family lived in a small village nestled on the beach of Ambon Island. Nus came from a Christian area, although his people maintained friendly relationships with nearby Muslim groups.

But the friendly climate changed when the Indonesian government began relocating foreign Muslims onto the island. The atmosphere became increasingly hostile.

One morning just before dawn, Muslim militants attacked the Christian villages. They came from all sides—from the sea in canoes, from the beach, and from behind the villages. They set fire to the buildings and used machetes, bamboo staves, and clubs to massacre the villagers. The attackers kept coming for a week, killing two hundred people. Thirty-eight of Nus's relatives died, including a brother, aunts, uncles, and cousins. Nus wept when he heard the names of the dead.

Grief sent Nus to his Indonesian Bible. He read from Psalm 119:68, "[God,] You are good and do only good." Nus decided God wanted him to forgive the militants who had caused so many such harm.

Although his people could not go back to their villages because of intimidation by the militant Muslims, Nus wanted to tell his enemies about the love of Jesus. "If I could talk to the killers," he said, "I wouldn't ask questions. Questions cause trouble. I would just tell them, 'Jesus loves you and has a wonderful plan for your life!' I would pray for them."[1]

Nus is an example of the strength of Jesus' love. This is not an emotional response but one that comes from Spirit-filled living. We can best discover this kind of love by looking at the heart of Jesus.

THE GREATEST LOVE

The Bible talks a lot about love. If you look up the word *love* in a Bible concordance, you will find many entries. The Bible even has a chapter that defines love. As you read the heart of this chapter, think about how it is a mirror image of the character of Jesus.

> Love is patient and kind. Love is not jealous or boastful or proud or rude. Love does not demand its own way. Love is not irritable, and it keeps no record of when it has been wronged. It is never glad about injustice but rejoices whenever the truth wins out. Love never gives up, never loses faith, is always hopeful, and endures through every circumstance. (1 Corinthians 13:4-7)

Let me point out just a few of the ways that Jesus showed us this kind of love.

- *Love is patient.* Jesus took so much time with people, even answering the questions of those who wanted to see Him fail.
- *Love is kind.* Jesus treated all people with respect and care, including lepers, immoral sinners, and the demon-possessed.
- *Love is not proud.* Jesus is God. He could have put on airs. He could have demanded worship. But He chose to be humble and willing.
- *Love does not demand its own way.* Jesus put the interests of others above His own. He took this attitude to its conclusion, finally sacrificing His life for us.
- *Love does not keep a record of wrongs.* When Jesus was suffering unjustly on the cross, facing ridicule from the mob and the soldiers, experiencing indescribable pain, He said, "Father, forgive these people, because they don't know what they are doing" (Luke 23:34).
- *Love endures through every circumstance.* Why didn't Jesus give up the plan to sacrifice His life when He agonized in the garden of Gethsemane? Because He suffered for our sake, out of love.

Jesus loved out of strength, not weakness. Paul writes, "There are three things that will endure—faith, hope, and love—and the greatest of these is love. Let love be your highest goal" (1 Corinthians 13:13–14:1). This perfectly describes Christ's purpose for being born as a man and dying for us!

THE PERFECT LOVE OF JESUS

Today the English word *love* has been terribly distorted. We hear expressions like

"I love chocolate."
"She fell out of love with her husband."
"Love means never having to say you're sorry."
"Ooh, I love it!"

We define *love* as a food craving, a fleeting emotion, or an almost meaningless exclamation. But the Greek language of the New Testament was much more specific about the definition of love. The Greek had three different words that all translate into the single word *love* in English.

- *Eros*—This word suggests sensual desire and does not appear in the New Testament.
- *Phileo*—This word refers to friendship or the love of one's friends or relatives. It conveys a sense of loving someone because he is worthy of love.
- *Agape*—This word describes God's love, the purest, deepest kind of love. It does not depend on feelings but is expressed through an act of the will. This love reflects the character of the person who loves rather than the worthiness of the person receiving the love.[2]

God's agape love is unconditional. Romans 5:10 explains, "We were restored to friendship with God by the death of His Son while we were still His enemies." God didn't begin to love you when you became His child by receiving Christ as your Savior. God *always* loved you. You were in His thoughts before He created the world. He loves the most wretched sinner. His love will never change, and you can never do anything to lessen His love for you.

Jesus is the highest expression of God's love. In Jesus, we have a real-life demonstration of how much God was willing to do for us in love.

Sometimes we may feel distant from God. We may even feel that He has removed Himself from us. That is a problem caused by you and me, not God. Either we have broken our fellowship with Him through unconfessed sin, or our fickle feelings are causing us to assess our situation wrongly.

But God's love never changes. You may not always feel it. You may feel disconnected from His love. You may feel that the situation you are in is so bad that God's love couldn't possibly reach you there. Listen to this promise God gives us concerning the love of Jesus:

> Can anything ever separate us from Christ's love? Does it mean He no longer loves us if we have trouble or calamity, or are persecuted, or are hungry or cold or in danger or threatened with death? . . . No, despite all these things, overwhelming victory is ours through Christ, Who loved us.
>
> And I am convinced that nothing can ever separate us from His love. Death can't, and life can't. The angels can't, and the demons can't. Our fears for today, our worries about tomorrow, and even the powers of hell can't keep God's love away. Whether we are high above the sky or in the deepest ocean, nothing in all creation will ever be able to separate us from the love of God that is revealed in Christ Jesus our Lord. (Romans 8:35-39)

Can you think of any problem that God doesn't address in this passage? When you feel isolated and alone, shut away from God, His love is still surrounding you. Your feelings may tell you that God doesn't love you anymore, but those feelings are wrong! You can have absolute assurance that nothing can come between you and the love of Jesus. In fact, Jesus says, "I have loved you even as the Father has loved Me" (John 15:9). Jesus loves you as much as His Father loves Him!

God's love is spread to us through the Holy Spirit living in us. Paul writes, "We know how dearly God loves us, because He has given us the Holy Spirit to fill our hearts with His love" (Romans 5:5). This is another reason why Spirit-filled living is so essential. As we allow the Holy Spirit to control us, He reveals how much God loves us.

THE COMMAND TO LOVE

We love others because God first loved us. "God is love, and all who live in love live in God, and God lives in them. . . . We love each other as a result of

His loving us first" (1 John 4:16, 19). God expects us to love others because we have benefited from His love.

We humans tend to alienate ourselves from each other through hurtful acts, hasty words, and other sins. Only God's universal love can break through the troublesome barriers that are created by human differences. Only a common devotion to Christ—the source of our love—can relieve tension, ease mistrust, encourage openness, bring out the best in people, and enable them to serve Christ in a more fruitful way.

One deep demonstration of God's kind of love comes from the life of Betsie ten Boom, a Dutch woman who, along with her sister Corrie, was sent to Nazi concentration camps for the crime of helping Jewish people escape death at the hands of the Nazis. Betsie was in her fifties when she and Corrie were assigned to Barracks 8 at the dreaded Ravensbruck concentration camp. When the sisters arrived, the conditions were horrific. Fourteen hundred women slept in a building built for four hundred. The women were beaten and tortured for the most minor infractions, and they were forced to do slave labor. When Corrie and Betsie settled into their places, Barracks 8 was a scene of fighting, cursing, and shoving among the starving and diseased prisoners. Betsie set out to show them God's love.

Every night, no matter how tired or sick she was, Betsie led a Bible study in the barracks. Women crowded around to hear her reading from the Bible that the sisters had miraculously smuggled into the prison camp. God's words were translated from woman to woman into German, French, Polish, Russian, and Czech. The atmosphere among the disease-ridden prisoners was transformed. Corrie writes, "What a difference since Betsie had come into this room! Where before this had been the moment for scuffle and cursing, tonight the huge dormitory buzzed with 'Sorry!' 'Excuse me!' and 'No harm done!'"[3]

Betsie's dream was to provide a place of healing for those who had suffered most during the war. She frequently described to Corrie the home filled with flowers and sunshine that she wanted to open for them. To Corrie's astonishment, Betsie's burden was not merely to help the women suffering around her. Betsie felt that the more tormented people in the camps were their persecutors, the guards, the ones who most desperately needed God's love![4]

That is the depth of love that Jesus Christ flows through us to others. He says, "I command you to love each other in the same way that I love you" (John 15:12). "You have heard that the law of Moses says, 'Love your neighbor' and hate your enemy. But I say, love your enemies! Pray for those who persecute you! In that way, you will be acting as true children of your Father in heaven" (Matthew 5:43-45).

But how can we do this? It's one thing to have such a lofty goal, but how do we put it into practice?

Love by Faith

How many times have you tried—and failed—to love an obstinate person? How often have you pasted a smile on your face when you met a difficult neighbor?

None of us is naturally patient and kind. Just as surely as we cannot please God in our own strength, we can't love as we should either. We like to demand our own way and take a little revenge now and then.

The answer is to love by faith.[5] Everything about the Christian life is based on faith. You love by faith just as you received Christ by faith, just as you are filled with the Holy Spirit by faith, and just as you walk by faith. Hebrews 11:6 says, "So, you see, it is impossible to please God without faith." Obviously, we cannot demonstrate God's love without faith.

If you have difficulty loving others, remember Jesus' command: "So now I am giving you a new commandment: Love each other. Just as I have loved you, you should love each other" (John 13:34). Therefore, it is God's will for you to love. He would not command you to do something that He will not enable you to do. God has an unending supply of His divine, supernatural agape love for you. It is for you to claim, to grow in, and to spread to others. To experience and share this love, you must claim it by faith; that is, you must trust His promise that He will give you all you need to do His will.

This truth is not new. It has been recorded in God's Word for two thousand years. But it was a new discovery to me one early morning some years ago when God showed me how to love. I began to practice loving by faith, and I found that problems I was having with other people seemed to disappear, often miraculously.

In one of those situations, I was having a difficult time loving a fellow staff member who was challenging my leadership role in the ministry. His attitude and actions troubled me. I wanted to love him. I knew that I was commanded to love him; yet because of certain areas of inconsistency and personality differences, it was difficult for me to love him. Then the Lord reminded me of 1 Peter 5:7, "Let Him have all your worries and cares, for He is always thinking about you and watching everything that concerns you" (TLB). I decided to give this problem to God and love this man by faith. When I claimed God's love for the man by faith, my concern lifted. I knew the matter was in God's hands.

An hour later, I found a letter under my door from that very man, who had no possible way of knowing what I had just experienced. In the letter, he asked me for forgiveness for challenging my leadership. The amazing thing was that his letter had been written the day before! The Lord had foreseen the change in me. This friend and I met that afternoon for the most wonderful time of prayer and fellowship we had ever experienced. Loving with God's love by faith had changed our relationship.

Take the Step

I encourage you to take the first step: Start loving by faith and follow that flow. You will find that God's compassion will stream through you toward a specific person in need. The tug of love within you means that He is filling you with godly compassion and that He has chosen you to minister to that person.

Ask God to manifest His tender compassion through you in some way today. As you pray, ask Him to lay someone on your heart. When you sense God's love flowing through you to that person, find out his or her need and begin ministering to that need. By following the leading of God's Spirit, you can help those whom the Lord has prepared for His transforming touch.

But what about those who seem especially unlikable? people who just "get your goat"? individuals who rub you the wrong way? I encourage you to make a list of people you do not like and begin to love them by faith. Perhaps you will place yourself on the list. Have you thought of applying the truths of 1 Corinthians 13 to yourself by faith? Ask God to help you see yourself as He sees you.

Then go to the others on your list. Perhaps your boss, a fellow employee, your spouse, your children, or your father or mother is on the list of those you want to love by faith. Pray for each person. Ask the Holy Spirit to fill you with Christ's love for all of them. Then seek to meet with them as you draw upon God's limitless love for them by faith. Expect God to work through you! Watch Him use your smile, your words, and your patience to express His love for each person.

Love by faith every one of your "enemies"—everyone who angers you, ignores you, bores you, or frustrates you. People are waiting to be loved with God's love.

Remember, agape love is an act of the will, not just an emotion. You love *by faith*. By faith you can claim God's love step-by-step, person-by-person.

How exciting to have such a dynamic, joyful force available to us! And it all comes from our loving Savior, Jesus Christ. This love is just the stepping-off point for what we can do for Him. As we spread His love, we will also learn how to lead others in Jesus' name.

Read about the Real Jesus: How can you become more loving?

> Love is patient and kind. Love is not jealous or boastful or proud
> or rude. Love does not demand its own way. Love is not irritable,
> and it keeps no record of when it has been wronged. It is never
> glad about injustice but rejoices whenever the truth wins out. Love
> never gives up, never loses faith, is always hopeful, and endures
> through every circumstance.
>
> 1 CORINTHIANS 13:4-7

1. What in this definition of love reminds you most of Jesus?

2. Do you know people who show this kind of love? What about them
   makes them so loving?

3. Think of a person who is hard for you to love. What unloving
   thoughts have you had about that person? What unloving things
   have you done? Confess those to God now.

4. Are you ready to love that person by faith? How will you take the
   first step?

5. How do you think your life will change when you put into practice
   the steps to loving by faith?

11

The Leadership of Jesus

*W*hat was Peter thinking the day that Jesus put him in one of the most awkward situations he'd ever faced? It happened after the Passover meal in the upper room. . . .

Peter felt a glow about him as he reclined after the meal. This had been an extraordinary day. Jesus was spending some exclusive time with the disciples. Peter looked around at the weatherworn faces of his friends. Matthew and John and Thomas were there, glad to be off the street and put up their feet for a while. The other disciples relaxed away from the table.

Peter watched as Jesus stood up. Were those lines of weariness around His eyes? Jesus slipped off His outer robe and laid it down. Peter leaned back, content.

Then Jesus wrapped a towel around His waist and picked up an empty basin from the table. He filled the basin with clean water from a pitcher.

Peter sat up straight when Jesus walked over to Thomas and knelt in front of him. Jesus gently picked up one of Thomas's feet and began washing it in the basin.

No one made a sound. This was incomprehensible! What was Jesus doing? Why would He stoop to wash Thomas's feet? He was the Master, the Son of God.

When Jesus finished washing, He carefully dried each foot with the towel He had wrapped around His waist. Then He moved on to John.

Peter glanced around at the other men. Wasn't someone going to say something? This was not proper. Jesus was their leader, not their slave.

As Jesus washed John's feet, Peter began to panic. He was next in line! He looked down at his dirt-encrusted feet. They smelled like the road. His toenails were split, and the skin was calloused. If he could just clean them a little before Jesus touched them. . . . He slipped his feet under his robe.

Jesus finished wiping John's feet and rose, carrying the basin with Him. He stood right in front of Peter, then knelt on one knee.

Well, someone had to stop Him! Peter exclaimed, "Lord, why are You going to wash my feet?" He tried to pull his feet further under his robe.

Jesus looked at Peter with those kind eyes. "You don't understand now why I am doing it; someday you will."

But Peter was determined to hold out. "No, You will never wash my feet!" He pulled the edge of his robe over his ankle.

Jesus' gaze was strong and unwavering. He held out His hand to touch Peter's foot. "But if I don't wash you, you won't belong to Me."

Peter looked up from his feet to Jesus' face. What was He saying? Was this some kind of test to see if Peter was loyal? Peter's mind roiled in a sea of confusion. "Then wash my hands and head as well, Lord, not just my feet!" (John 13:9). He stuck out both of his feet and pulled his robe back to his knees. Instantly, by the look on Jesus' face, Peter knew he had said the wrong thing.

Jesus began to wash. The water trickled down Peter's ankle in a little rivulet of coolness. Jesus spoke. "A person who has bathed all over does not need to wash, except for the feet, to be entirely clean. And you are clean" (John 13:10).

Slowly, Jesus finished washing and drying Peter's feet. They felt so relaxed after the Master's touch. Then Jesus moved on to the next person.

The room remained completely silent while Jesus finished His work. Then He set the basin on the table and removed the towel. He turned back to look at His friends, who had such confused expressions on their faces.

Peter waited. Now perhaps Jesus would explain.

"Do you understand what I was doing?" [Jesus asked]. "You call me 'Teacher' and 'Lord,' and you are right, because it is true. And since I, the Lord and Teacher, have washed your feet, you ought to wash each other's feet. I have given you an example to follow. Do as I have done to you. How true it is that a servant is not greater than the master. Nor are messengers more important than the one who sends them. You know these things—now do them! That is the path of blessing" (John 13:12-17).[1]

How would you have felt if you had been sitting in Peter's place? How would you react right now if Jesus walked into the room, removed your shoes, and started washing your feet? Would you protest? get so embarrassed that you couldn't talk?

Just what was the lesson that Jesus was teaching us through His example? If we are to be leaders in God's Kingdom, we must be servants. This principle has far-reaching effects on our lives. And the lesson comes from the heart of Jesus, who lived a life of servanthood to benefit us all.

SERVANT OF GOD

In the Old Testament, the Messiah is called God's servant. In Isaiah 52:13, God says, "See, My servant will prosper; He will be highly exalted." This seems like such a contradiction! How can a lowly servant prosper? He has neither the position nor the resources. This mystery of the Messiah's position is brought out even more clearly in Isaiah 52:14-15: "Many were amazed when they saw Him—beaten and bloodied, so disfigured one would scarcely know He was a person. And He will again startle many nations. Kings will stand speechless in His presence. For they will see what they had not previously been told about; they will understand what they had not heard about."

What a mixed bag of images God gives us in these two passages. The servant will be a ruler. The persecuted one will be a king. How can these things all exist in the same person?

This mystery is explained in Philippians 2:5-11:

Your attitude should be the same that Christ Jesus had. Though
He was God, He did not demand and cling to His rights as God.
He made Himself nothing; He took the humble position of a slave
and appeared in human form. And in human form He obediently
humbled Himself even further by dying a criminal's death on a cross.
Because of this, God raised Him up to the heights of heaven and gave
Him a name that is above every other name, so that at the name of
Jesus every knee will bow, in heaven and on earth and under the
earth, and every tongue will confess that Jesus Christ is Lord, to the
glory of God the Father.

Just as Jesus has called us to love others as He loves us, He also asks us to serve others as He served us. In fact, He tells us that our servant hearts will be the distinction that marks us as leaders in God's Kingdom.

The disciples had a hard time grasping this lesson. One day the brothers James and John came to Jesus with their mother, who asked Him to set her two sons in the places of favor in His Kingdom. Jesus then gave His followers the principle for achieving leadership positions in God's realm: "You know that in this world kings are tyrants, and officials lord it over the people beneath them. But among you it should be quite different. Whoever wants to be a leader among you must be your servant, and whoever wants to be first must become your slave. For even I, the Son of Man, came here not to be served but to serve others, and to give My life as a ransom for many" (Matthew 20:25-28).

This concept of servant leadership is so foreign to us that we may not even know how to begin practicing it. You may be wondering, does it mean that I have to be a doormat for others' demands? How will I know what attitude to have? What's in it for me?

Just like every other principle Jesus taught, we can look at His life to find our answers.

The Sacrificial Servant

The last verse of the passage from Matthew quoted above tells us the purpose of Jesus' life—to give His life as a ransom for us. This is the ultimate in Jesus' example of leadership. He saw that we were doomed to eternal death unless He provided a way for our redemption. He was willing to give His all—His very life—for the most unworthy sinner. That means you and me. He led by giving up His life.

What are you willing to do in return? What will you sacrifice for the sake of Jesus? Many before us have shown us how to give all for the sake of others, as Jesus has asked us to do.

The story of two of the greatest heroes for Christ in recent times comes out of the "killing fields" of Cambodia, where Vek Huong Taing and his wife, Samouen, ministered. I consider it the greatest privilege to know them and to have them as part of our Campus Crusade for Christ staff family.

The couple was in Phnom Penh just before Pol Pot began his reign of terror and carnage in Cambodia. Our Asian director, Dr. Bailey Marks, notified Huong by telex of the danger and advised him to leave the country.

Huong answered that he and his wife and infant son would stay with their people until the last days of their lives. The desire of their hearts was to reach as many Cambodians as possible with the gospel of Jesus.

A few days later, Cambodia fell to Pol Pot. For four years, no one outside Cambodia knew what had happened to the Taing family. We didn't know if they were alive or dead. In that period of time, more than 1.5 million Cambodians were tortured and killed.

Vek Huong and Samouen and their son endured unbelievable privation. They resorted to eating the skin and the heads of rats to stay alive. They traded baby clothes for food. They made a pact that whether they were separated or were able to stay together, whether they lived or died, they would serve their Lord.

Through a series of miracles, the family was able to make their way to a refugee camp in Thailand. There Huong was interviewed by a Reuters reporter from England, and in a short time our offices in Asia were informed that the Taings were alive. You can imagine our joy!

What was their desire after suffering so deeply? To go back to Cambodia and help the hurting Cambodian people find peace in Christ![2] Vek Huong and Samouen truly exemplify the servant heart and leadership of Jesus.

We, too, can sacrifice for Jesus where we are. We may not have the privilege of giving our lives for Him or enduring severe persecution, but we can serve Him in many ways. When we put others first and desire to tell them about Jesus, we follow His example of servant leadership. Let's look at some characteristics of a servant that Jesus showed us: being humble, encouraging, and giving.

The Humble Servant

A servant has a humble position. Philippians 2:5-11 describes the humility of Jesus: "He took the humble position of a slave and appeared in human form" (v. 7). He endured ridicule and shame and death as a criminal for us.

Do you see yourself as a humble person? We laugh about people who claim to be "humble and proud of it!" But humility is a serious issue to the Christian. We cannot mix the attitudes of servanthood and pride. They are polar opposites.

Being humble means surrendering our own rights to serve others, just as Jesus did. It means being willing to serve without any recognition if necessary.

One of the remarkable qualities of Steve Douglass, the new president of

Campus Crusade for Christ, is humility. He worked closely with me for thirty-one years before being named president. No matter what he has been asked to do, he has responded with the spirit of a servant. Steve could have taken countless other high-profile jobs—I know he has been offered many. But he chose to stay with our ministry in what many consider to be a low-profile role because he has a heart to see the world won for Christ.

God sees all those who serve Him—whether they are famous or not. When we all meet later in heaven, we will recognize the many servants of the Lord who worked quietly on this earth for God's glory: the young father in a rural church who gives up his time to mentor boys who are needy; the elderly invalid who dedicates her remaining days to a deep prayer ministry; those who give up what little they have in their bank account so that others can go and tell about Jesus; the missionary who works in a corner of the world with no news media. Our list could go on and on. God sees their hearts and rewards their humble spirits.

The Encouraging Servant

Have you noticed how Jesus carefully taught His disciples what they needed to know about God and how to serve Him? His careful training, constant presence, and kind words encouraged them to be God's servants as well.

I think of the example Jesus gave His disciples for ministering in small villages. Up until then, they had watched Him talk to a variety of people. He spoke patiently, addressed the person's needs, and turned them toward God. Now it was time for the disciples to do what He had taught them. He gathered them together and paired them up (see Mark 6:6-13; Luke 9:1-6). He explained what they were to do and say. Then He gave them the power to cast out demons and heal the sick. He instructed them to tell the people to repent. He was a hands-on teacher.

This is the pattern of ministry that the apostles often used when beginning the early church. In Acts 3 Peter and John healed a man in the Temple, then Peter preacheed about Jesus. In Acts 13 Paul and Barnabas went on the first missionary journey. They traveled from town to town, telling people about the Good News. Silas accompanied Paul on his second missionary journey (Acts 16). They followed the example that Jesus had set for them.

In so many other ways, Jesus encouraged His followers to develop godly, Spirit-filled lives. He also does that for us as we yield ourselves to Him. He then asks us to pass on His example of encouragement and mentoring to people we touch.

The Giving Servant

Paul writes about Jesus: "You know how full of love and kindness our Lord Jesus Christ was. Though He was very rich, yet for your sakes He became poor, so that by His poverty He could make you rich" (2 Corinthians 8:9). How rich do you feel because of Jesus? What has He given you? He has given us eternal life, peace with God, His divine friendship and protection, and so many other gifts that we could never purchase on our own. He provided all this by living as a pauper on earth. He gave up everything for our benefit.

A giving servant sees the needs of the person whom others overlook. Jesus used a child to teach His disciples about serving the least among us. Once again the disciples were arguing about who among them was greatest. They still figured that Jesus was going to set up an earthly kingdom in Jerusalem, and they each wanted a big piece of the kingdom pie.

This is what Jesus told them: "Anyone who wants to be the first must take last place and be the servant of everyone else" (Mark 9:35). Then He took a child in His arms. "Anyone who welcomes a little child like this on My behalf welcomes Me, and anyone who welcomes Me welcomes My Father who sent Me" (v. 37).

This is the link. Whenever you give to someone who is helpless or needy, you are serving Jesus and, in turn, the Father. In addition, I can tell you from personal experience that serving those who can't repay you brings the deepest satisfaction.

Several years ago, Vonette and I were about to celebrate our wedding anniversary. I was trying to think of a special, elegant place to take her that would express how important she is to me. I wanted it to be a meaningful evening.

But something happened that changed my mind. After discussing the plans with Vonette, we agreed that instead of going to an elegant hotel, we would go to skid row and serve meals to the homeless. We knew a friend who ran a kitchen for the homeless, so he arranged for us to go.

Soon after we arrived, we were given our assigned places in the serving line, and people began walking by cafeteria-style. Right away I noticed that these people carried an air of defeat. No one looked me in the eye. I found myself identifying with them. I thought, *But for the grace of God, what happened to them could happen to me,* and I began to weep.

I served for an entire hour with tears streaming down my cheeks. I thought about the compassion Jesus had for people as He ministered to them. I recalled the verse in Matthew 9:36: "[Jesus] felt great pity for the crowds that came, because their problems were so great and they didn't know where to go for help." The experience at the homeless kitchen gave me a deeper compassion for people who are less fortunate than I am. Anyone could have served those meals, but God wanted me to give up my time so that I could receive a message from Him—the importance of being a servant.

THE REWARD OF A SERVANT

Perhaps you are reluctant to follow the pattern of Jesus and live as a servant. You may feel that you will become a shoeless missionary with nothing but a Bible and the promise of eternal rewards. Perhaps you are worried about not having any will of your own.

Dear friend, nothing could be further from the truth. When you are a servant of God, and consequently of others, it is amazing how God provides for your needs and blesses you with overflowing abundance.

Since 1951, Vonette and I have dedicated our talents, treasures, and time to help fulfill the Great Commission of our Lord. Today, by choice, we possess little of this world's goods because we feel God has called us to a higher purpose—to be His servants. We have directed our desires away from material things, and yet God has always, without our effort or our seeking, provided us with incredible blessings.

One such blessing has been the places we have lived during our fifty years of marriage. For ten years we enjoyed a wonderful ministry at the heart of the UCLA campus in fabulous Bel Air, California. Then we spent thirty-two years at Arrowhead Springs, California, which is one of the most beautiful places in the world. Ever since then, we have lived in Orlando, Florida, a place of prestige and beauty, comfort and convenience. Although we have never owned a house of our own, I am amazed at what God has provided for us as we willingly served Him.

I'm not suggesting that because you choose to live as a servant of God you can expect to be surrounded by riches. Many of God's servants work in primitive and remote places of the world and do not have the amenities that we enjoy in the Western world. Yet they truly love and honor the Lord as much as Vonette and I do. Whatever their circumstances, they rejoice because God is faithful. They see how God supplies their needs. They see how He blesses them in unique ways that fit their work and situation.

But what about the world's idea that being a servant means living as a human doormat? Jesus does not expect us to serve at the whims of anyone. When we do that, we supplant God's authority. Instead, we should look to God for our directions, then obey the authorities He places above us. We should be aware of people's needs, but we also need to realize that God is ultimately responsible for people's lives. We are merely His managers on earth, serving under His command. Our blessing arises from pleasing God, not from merely pleasing people.

Any person in full-time ministry will tell you that the needs are so great, ministry may destroy the well-being of the one who serves. Therefore, God expects us to live in balance. Keep your eyes focused on Jesus. Remember that He took time away from the crowds to rest and be refreshed.

Early in my ministry, God laid on my heart the burden of reaching the whole world with the Good News of Jesus. No one person can accomplish this task—it could easily overwhelm anyone. But I realize that I am just a small part of God's plan. So I respond to the needs of others, but I do it under the guidance of the Holy Spirit.

If we follow Jesus' example of service, God promises to reward us. Paul writes, "Work hard and cheerfully at whatever you do, as though you were working for the Lord rather than for people. Remember that the Lord will give you an inheritance as your reward, and the Master you are serving is Christ" (Colossians 3:23-24).

We will not see all our rewards in this life, but we can be sure that God sees our servant attitude and will bless us now and in the future. I have experienced so many intangible rewards from God: the comradeship of wonderful believers, working together in ministry with Vonette, the unbelievable joy of seeing lives change, the satisfaction of seeing God work in me to make me more like Jesus. But most of all, I experience the joy and satisfaction of serving our wonderful Lord and Master, who deserves my total commitment. That is my greatest reward.

Discover Jesus

Read about the Real Jesus: How can you obey Jesus' instructions?

> I have given you an example to follow. Do as I have done to you.
> How true it is that a servant is not greater than the master. Nor are
> messengers more important than the one who sends them. You
> know these things—now do them! That is the path of blessing.
>
> JOHN 13:15-17

1. After learning about all that Jesus has done for you, how do you
   feel about serving Him?

2. How have you seen Christians serve others?

3. What have you learned from their examples?

4. What opportunities do you have to serve others?

5. Ask God daily to give you a servant attitude as you lead others.

12

The Obedience of Jesus

*F*or the fifth time in three months, officers burst into the room where fifty people were worshipping. One of the officers found Pastor Li and struck him across his face, throwing the diminutive man to the ground. The other officers joined the fracas, kicking Pastor Li and hitting him with their batons. While the lead officer roughly handcuffed the pastor and carried him off to jail, the other officers began cuffing the remaining worshippers. The scene was not new to them. They knew that their obedience to Jesus Christ might cost them their lives, but they had counted the cost. These believers were willing to pay the price.

Charlene stood resolute in her boss's office. He had just asked her to falsify financial records so that their company would not need to declare bankruptcy. "Bob, I can't do what you've asked me to do. I'm a Christian, and I refuse to participate in this kind of dishonesty."

"Charlene, you don't have an option here," her boss insisted. "Either you do what I ask, or you look for another job. I'm serious."

By that afternoon Charlene cleared out her desk and walked out of the office building where she had worked for sixteen years. Even though she needed the income very badly to pay for her son's medical care, she knew she needed to obey God's standards even more.

What made these people endure pain and loss? When one of Charlene's friends questioned her decision to walk away from her job, Charlene explained, "Janeen, I know it sounds foolish to you that I wouldn't fudge a little on Bob's records. You may be right that even if Bob were caught, I would not be held accountable. But you need to understand that my commitment to Jesus Christ is very important to me. My loyalty to Him is much deeper than my loyalty to a boss. Just a few weeks ago our Bible study group studied Acts 5, a chapter that describes how Peter and the apostles were commanded by the local government authorities to stop preaching about Jesus. The apostles disregarded the command, believing that it was more important to obey God than it was to obey human authority. Well, that's what I felt like saying to Bob: 'I must obey God rather than you.' Yes, it cost me my job, but I know I did the right thing."

What gave Charlene and the Chinese Christians the strength to obey in the face of persecution and loss? The example of Jesus Himself.

In history's most powerful moment of obedience and love, Jesus Christ willingly submitted to a gruesome, excruciating crucifixion to satisfy His Father's demand that someone had to pay the price for sin. Jesus Christ unflinchingly paid our debt, even though it cost Him everything. The apostle Paul describes this obedience like this: "[Jesus], being in very nature God, did not consider equality with God something to be grasped, but made himself nothing, taking the very nature of a servant, being made in human likeness. . . . He humbled himself and became obedient to death—even death on a cross!" (Philippians 2:6-8, NIV).

With an example like that, committed Christians gain the courage to face their own tests of obedience, no matter what the cost. They embrace the words of Colossians 2:6-7: "Just as you accepted Christ Jesus as your Lord, you must continue to live in obedience to Him. Let your roots grow down into Him and draw up nourishment from Him, so you will grow in faith, strong and vigorous in the truth you were taught." Followers of Christ draw their nourishment from His example of utter obedience to His Father. They dare to obey.

WHY WAS CHRIST'S OBEDIENCE IMPORTANT?

When Jesus lived on earth, He never did anything on His own. Every decision, every action, He did at the direction of His Father. Why did Jesus, who was Himself God, place Himself in a position of obedience? The Bible gives us several reasons.

1. Jesus obeyed because He wanted to make people right with God. Jesus' goal was to reconcile sinful people with a holy God. The only way He could do that was by obeying the Father's plan for redemption. The New Testament reminds us, "Yes, Adam's one sin brought condemnation upon everyone, but Christ's one act of righteousness makes all people right in God's sight and gives them life. Because one person disobeyed God, many people became sinners. But because one other person obeyed God, many people will be made right in God's sight" (Romans 5:18-19). Jesus didn't come on His own; the Father sent Him. Jesus was an obedient Son.

2. Jesus obeyed because the prophets predicted He would. Jesus said to His Father, "You did not want animal sacrifices and grain offerings. But You have given Me a body so that I may obey You. No, You were not pleased with animals burned on the altar or with other offerings for sin. Then I said, 'Look, I have come to do Your will, O God—just as it is written about Me in the Scriptures'" (Hebrews 10:5-7).

Even before Jesus was born, the prophets predicted that He would come to do the Father's will. Jesus willingly placed Himself in the position of doing whatever the Father asked, and He thereby fulfilled the prophecies concerning the Messiah. (Read Isaiah 53 to see how Jesus did exactly as the Father had commissioned Him to do.)

3. Jesus obeyed to show the world that He loved His Father. If you are a parent, you know how much it pleases you when your children obey your requests and rules. Their obedience demonstrates their love and respect for you; their disobedience, on the other hand, clearly reflects their disrespect.

Jesus wanted the world to know that He loved His Father. This is what Jesus said about His witness to the world, "I will do what the Father requires of Me, so that the world will know that I love the Father" (John 14:31). Jesus knew that His obedience to the Father—to the point of death—was one of the most powerful testimonies of their relationship.

Obviously, if Jesus obeyed the Father, so should we. In fact, Jesus modeled obedience for us so that we would know how to obey our heavenly Father.

JESUS EXPECTED OBEDIENCE

Have you ever worked for people who expected higher standards for their employees than they did for themselves? They expect you to be at your desk at eight o'clock in the morning, but they float in at nine. They excuse you from work only when you have an emergency in your family, but they go home to supervise workers in their houses or to meet friends. They do minimal repairs on the plumbing in the employees' restrooms, but they lavishly decorate their own offices.

Jesus never expected more of His followers than He asked of Himself. So when the Bible shows that He asked others to obey Him completely, they were more than willing to accept. When He called His disciples, they followed Him immediately:

> One day as Jesus was walking along the shore beside the Sea of Galilee, He saw two brothers—Simon, also called Peter, and Andrew—fishing with a net, for they were commercial fishermen. Jesus called out to them, "Come be My disciples, and I will show you how to fish for people!" And they left their nets at once and went with Him.
>
> A little farther up the shore He saw two other brothers, James and John, sitting in a boat with their father, Zebedee, mending their nets. And He called them to come, too. They immediately followed Him, leaving the boat and their father behind. (Matthew 4:18-22)

Can you imagine what Zebedee must have thought! But his sons had no questions about Jesus. They wanted to be near Him and to do what He said.

Many times, Jesus tested His disciples' obedience and rewarded them for obeying. Once, after His resurrection, the disciples were fishing. Perhaps they didn't know what to do with themselves now that Jesus was gone, so they went back to their old standby. They fished all night, but caught nothing.

When the sun came up, they saw someone standing on the shore, but they couldn't make out who it was. The man said, "Friends, have you caught any fish?"

"No," they replied.

Then Jesus gave them an odd instruction. "Throw out your net on the right-hand side of the boat, and you'll get plenty of fish!"

What kind of suggestion was that? How could there be more fish on one side of a boat than the other—especially since they hadn't caught any fish all night, no matter where they sailed? But they obeyed, and they caught so many fish that they couldn't draw in their nets.

At once, the disciples recognized Jesus. Impetuous Peter immediately jumped into the water and swam to shore. The other disciples rowed in the boat. When they got to shore, they smelled the fish that Jesus was frying for them over a fire (see John 21:1-9). Not only did the disciples spend time eating with Jesus, but they also had an enormous catch of fish to sell!

ATTITUDES OF OBEDIENCE

The Bible describes heart attitudes that should accompany our obedience to God. These attitudes please God and enrich our lives.

Our obedience should be *wholehearted*. When Moses taught the Israelite people about obedience to God, he said, "Today the Lord your God has commanded you to obey all these laws and regulations. You must commit yourself to them without reservation" (Deuteronomy 26:16).

What happens if you obey traffic laws halfheartedly? If you occasionally wander over the solid lines in the middle of the road, you may eventually be involved in a head-on collision. What about the law of gravity? Would you ever walk off the edge of a cliff? No, we obey the law of gravity wholeheartedly. Why then do we consider God's eternal laws so flimsy that we often obey them only halfheartedly? God has given us His moral laws for our well-being. We must obey them with all our hearts!

Sometimes obedience takes *courage*. In the Old Testament Joshua faced a daunting task. He had to lead the people of Israel into a hostile land. But God had promised them success if they obeyed Him. He told them, "Be strong and very courageous. Obey all the laws Moses gave you. Do not turn away from them, and you will be successful in everything you do" (Joshua 1:7). Because of Joshua's obedience, he was successful in battle.

Which of God's commands takes courage for you to follow? Telling others about Jesus? Doing the right thing at work when everyone else is cutting ethical corners? Speaking up for God's principles in your college classroom? Keeping on with your ministry when you feel incredibly discouraged?

Obedience to God takes *commitment*. Our obedience should take precedence over everything else. When Peter and the apostles were arrested and accused of violating the rule of not speaking the name of Jesus, they said, "We must obey God rather than human authority" (Acts 5:29).

Most of the apostles paid with their lives for obeying God rather than the authorities of their day. The New Testament tells us that James was executed by King Agrippa. Tradition says that Matthew was martyred with a spear in the city of Nadabah in AD 60. Andrew was crucified in Patras, Greece. Thomas was martyred with a spear in India. And Peter was crucified upside down in Rome. They were all obeying Christ's command to tell the world about Him (see Matthew 28:18-20), and they faced their future with joy. Through the centuries, so many others have given their lives and possessions to obey Jesus. We can do no less.

This is the principle of obedience that God gives us: "Obedience is far better than sacrifice" (1 Samuel 15:22). In other words, we can spend hours in worship or any other religious activity, but if we aren't obeying God wholeheartedly our worship is empty. We can give up things for God's sake, but if we aren't obeying God courageously our sacrifice is worth nothing. What Jesus modeled and God expects is our commitment to Him first.

Academy Award nominee Gary Busey learned the importance of obedience the hard way. He grew up in a Christian home but never turned his life over to Jesus. When he announced to his father that he was going to Hollywood to make music, his father answered, "You can do everything through Christ."

In Hollywood, the Oklahoma boy didn't find a place in music, but he got a break in acting. He was cast in *High Chaparral* and *Kung Fu* in the late 1960s and 1970s. He brags, "I was the last man killed on *Gunsmoke*." In 1978, he landed the leading role in *The Buddy Holly Story* and received an Oscar nomination. He was on top of the film world.

But Busey's success was marred by a cocaine addiction, which had a grip on his life. However, years later, Busey attended a Promise Keepers rally in Los Angeles and rushed to the front to turn his life over to Christ. When Busey returned home, his wife, who had nicknamed him "Gary Abusey," noticed the change in his life.

In August 1997, Busey spoke to fans at a church in Tulsa, Oklahoma. He told the audience, "A star is simply a self-contained mass of gas. I am not a star; I am a Christian." Today, Busey has the courage to share his faith with his friends in the entertainment industry. "I am proud to tell Hollywood I am a Christian," he says. "For the first time I am free to be myself."[1]

That's what obedience does for us. It frees us to be all that Jesus wants us to be. Because Jesus was obedient, He could be our Savior and High Priest. Because I am obedient, I can reach the potential that God plans for my life. Our obedience makes us like Jesus:

- Like Jesus, my obedience allows me to bring people to God so that they can be reconciled with their heavenly Father.

- Like Jesus, I am a child of God and can please my Father through my obedience.

- Like Jesus, my obedience shows the world how much I love God.

- Like Jesus, my obedience keeps the love communion open between my heavenly Father and me.

- And like Jesus, my obedience qualifies me to work in God's kingdom in the position He has ordained for me.

And best of all, God blesses those who obey Him. One of the New Testament writers instructed us: "If you keep looking steadily into God's perfect law—the law that sets you free—and if you do what it says and don't forget what you heard, then God will bless you for doing it" (James 1:25).

Don't you desire the life of obedience and the blessings that follow? Spirit-filled living is the power for obedience. Studying God's Word is the map for obedience. Jesus is our example. We have everything we need!

Discover Jesus

Read about the Real Jesus: Hear what Jesus said about obedience:

> Those who obey My commandments are the ones who love Me.
> And because they love Me, My Father will love them, and I will love
> them. And I will reveal Myself to each one of them.
>
> JOHN 14:21

1. What does our obedience to God reveal about us?

2. According to this verse, what blessing does our obedience reap?

3. In what areas do you have difficulty obeying God?

4. What kinds of consequences have you reaped because of your lack
   of obedience?

5. What kinds of blessings might you see if you changed your
   disobedience into obedience in these areas?

6. In what specific areas will you commit to obeying God
   wholeheartedly?

13

The Prayers of Jesus

I learned a valuable lesson early in my ministry: Prayer is essential. For more than a year before Campus Crusade for Christ began, I led church teams into college dormitories, fraternities, and sororities in the Los Angeles area. My heart was in the right place; I had a desire to introduce college students to Jesus. But as far as I know, not a single person committed his or her life to Christ at any of these meetings.

But when God called this ministry into being in the spring of 1951, we immediately formed a twenty-four-hour prayer chain and divided the prayer time into ninety-six fifteen-minute periods. Scores of Christians invested fifteen minutes in prayer every day on behalf of our new ministry at the University of California at Los Angeles.

What happened? During the very first sorority meeting at UCLA after the prayer chain began, more than half of the sixty women present expressed a desire to receive Christ as their Savior. Over the next few months, more than 250 students at UCLA—including the president of the student body, the editor of the college newspaper, and a number of top athletes— committed their lives to Jesus Christ. So great was their influence for Christ that the campus chimes began to play Christian hymns at noon each day!

This unprecedented demonstration of God's blessing was no accident.

God was responding to the prayers of many of His children. I learned that my own efforts at doing God's will amounted to nothing, but when I worked through the power of prayer, the results were miraculous. God's blessing continues to this day as He is using Campus Crusade for Christ to help introduce tens of millions of people to our Savior and to build disciples in all the major countries of the world. Prayer continues to be our major emphasis.

As I grew in my faith in those early days and learned more about our wonderful Savior, I discovered how important prayer was to Jesus when He lived on earth. Why is that true? Because prayer is the link Jesus used to communicate with His own Father. And He expected His followers to do the same.

THE PRAYER EXAMPLE OF JESUS

Do you know how often Jesus prayed? Many Scripture passages give us information about His prayer life.

Jesus often took time alone to talk to His Father. Mark writes, "The next morning Jesus awoke long before daybreak and went out alone into the wilderness to pray" (1:35). Another time when the disciples were in a boat, Jesus spent the time in prayer. "Afterward He went up into the hills by Himself to pray" (Mark 6:46). In fact, the New Testament tells us that Jesus had a habit of going off alone to pray. Luke says, "But Jesus often withdrew to the wilderness for prayer" (5:16).

Not only did Jesus find a quiet place to pray, He spent long periods of time conversing with the Father. In Luke 6:12-13, Jesus went to a mountain to pray all night. He did this just before He selected twelve men to be His disciples. During this prayer time, He must have been discussing with His Father what He was about to do.

Prayer was also an important part of Jesus' public ministry. He began His ministry at His baptism. The communication between the three Persons of the Trinity at that moment was clear to everyone. Luke describes what happened: "One day when the crowds were being baptized, Jesus Himself was baptized [by John the Baptist]. As He was praying, the heavens opened, and the Holy Spirit descended on Him in the form of a dove. And a voice from heaven said, 'You are My beloved Son, and I am fully pleased with You'" (3:21-22).

Do you notice the communication between the Son, the Father, and the Holy Spirit? It all began as Jesus was praying.

We read earlier how Jesus prayed all night right before He called His disciples. He was also praying during His transfiguration. That was when His appearance changed into the form He would have after His resurrection. "About eight days later Jesus took Peter, James, and John to a mountain to pray. And as He was praying, the appearance of His face changed, and His clothing became dazzling white. Then two men, Moses and Elijah, appeared and began talking with Jesus. They were glorious to see. And they were speaking of how He was about to fulfill God's plan by dying in Jerusalem" (Luke 9:28-31).

At this time, God the Father once again spoke from heaven. "This is My Son, My Chosen One. Listen to Him" (vs. 35).

And Jesus certainly relied on communication with His Father throughout the ordeal of the cross. We read about how He prayed for His followers in the garden of Gethsemane. He also poured out His agony to His Father. He fell on His face and said, "My Father! If it is possible, let this cup of suffering be taken away from Me. Yet I want Your will, not Mine" (Matthew 26:39).

Jesus prayed while He was on the cross. He said, "Father, forgive these people, because they don't know what they are doing" (Luke 23:34). And at the last moment of His life, He shouted, "Father, I entrust My spirit into Your hands!" (Luke 23:46). Then He died. His work was done.

Jesus undoubtedly prayed many more times than what was recorded in the Gospels. But these examples were given to us so that we could understand the depth of the communion between Father and Son.

THE HIGH PRIEST AND PRAYER

In the Old Testament, a priest was chosen to represent the people's dealings with God. The priests offered the sacrifices in the Temple, including incense, which represented the prayer of the saints going up to God. The high priest was the only person allowed to step into the Most Holy Place in the Temple. He entered the Most Holy Place once a year to offer a blood sacrifice on the altar inside.

The Old Testament high priest foreshadowed the work of Jesus in dying on the cross for sin. The Book of Hebrews explains:

Nothing in all creation can hide from [God]. Everything is naked and exposed before His eyes. This is the God to whom we must explain all that we have done. That is why we have a great High Priest who has gone to heaven, Jesus the Son of God. Let us cling to Him and never stop trusting Him. This High Priest of ours understands our weaknesses, for He faced all of the same temptations we do, yet He did not sin. So let us come boldly to the throne of our gracious God. There we will receive His mercy, and we will find grace to help us when we need it. (4:13-16)

This is what is happening in heaven right now. Jesus is sitting next to the throne of the Father, serving as a mediator between God and us.

Why is Jesus such a good go-between? Because He understands our weaknesses and our temptations. He experienced it all when He lived on earth. Yet because He never sinned, He can communicate perfectly with His Father. Doesn't that give you confidence about the effectiveness of your prayer life?

THE WONDERFUL NAME OF JESUS

Would you believe that each time you pray, the entire Trinity is involved in your requests? This is what the Bible tells us:

1. God the Father hears and answers our prayers. Jesus said, "When you pray, go away by yourself, shut the door behind you, and pray to your Father secretly. Then your Father, who knows all secrets, will reward you" (Matthew 6:6).

2. Jesus the Son is our mediator. Jesus said, "You can ask for anything in My name, and I will do it" (John 14:13).

3. The Holy Spirit helps us pray. "The Holy Spirit helps us in our distress. For we don't even know what we should pray for, nor how we should pray. But the Holy Spirit prays for us with groanings that cannot be expressed in words" (Romans 8:26).

Isn't it amazing that each time you pray, all three Persons of the Trinity are involved? They all want us to pray. The Bible tells us that Jesus is in heaven right now, sitting at the right hand of the Father, helping us get our prayers answered. Our response should be to talk to God in prayer often.

Because Jesus is our High Priest, we pray in His name. When the Father hears the name of His beloved Son, He listens. John 14:13 tells us to pray in Jesus' name. Jesus is not only the way to God for our salvation but also our mediator in prayer so that we can confidently come before God. We owe everything to Jesus.

Jesus taught us the principles of prayer. Using them brings us to the center of heaven.

Jesus' Teachings about Prayer

Can you imagine what it must have been like to learn how to pray at the feet of Jesus as the disciples did? Jesus prayed with them. They saw His prayers turn into miracles. They were with Him when He poured out His heart in agony to His Father.

We see how important Jesus considered prayer by looking at what He taught on the subject. You are probably most familiar with Jesus' teaching called the Lord's Prayer. Early in His ministry, Jesus taught the disciples how to pray. First He gave them some do's and don'ts of prayer in Matthew 6:5-8:

- Don't pray to show off.
- Do pray in secret.
- Don't pray repetitious words.
- Do expect God to answer.

Then Jesus gave the disciples a model prayer that they could use when they formed their own prayers. This is the Lord's Prayer (see Matthew 6:9-13). Over the centuries Christians all over the world have learned it and loved it.

We know how to pray because Jesus left us many teachings about prayer:

Jesus tells us to pray constantly and to never give up. Jesus told his disciples the story of the persistent widow to teach that it's important to keep on praying, even if we don't see immediate results (see Luke 18:1-8). Jennifer Edwards knew the value of persistent prayer. Jennifer Edwards is a student at The School of the Art Institute of Chicago, a prestigious school that has never had a Christian group on campus. When she arrived, she felt led to start one. But she didn't even know one other Christian student. And the climate at the college was definitely not sympathetic to Christianity. But she put up some fliers inviting students to a Campus Crusade for Christ meeting.

A teacher's assistant noticed the flier in a hallway. "Who the [obscenity] would put that up at a school like this?" he shouted.

Jennifer bravely said, "I did."

"I don't ever want you to look at me in the eye again!" the man said as he stomped off.

Jennifer found that starting the ministry was incredibly difficult. For the first year and a half, the best support was her sister, who was involved with a similar ministry on the University of Iowa campus. Jennifer also met frequently with a Campus Crusade staff member, Ana, who worked in the Chicago area, and together they prayed and wept over the art campus. Soon after, other students joined Jennifer, and the newly formed Christian group gained official recognition by the college. Today, these courageous students are an example to other Christian groups on other campuses. All because Jennifer and her friends prayed rather than gave up.[1] That is the attitude of prayer that Jesus desires of us.

Jesus expects us to pray in faith. Jesus taught His disciples. "If you believe, you will receive whatever you ask for in prayer" (Matthew 21:22). Prayer offered in faith sees results. Throughout my life and ministry I have seen the direct relationship between faith and answered prayer.

A number of years ago, a terrible brush fire threatened the grounds of what then served as our conference center, Arrowhead Springs in California. Many buildings, including the bungalow where Vonette and I lived, came extremely close to being engulfed in flames. Seven of the buildings were destroyed.

It's hard to describe the horror of these California fires. They burn hot and quick, licking up everything in their paths. The canyons and washes are so steep that it's hard for firefighters to combat the flames. The Santa Ana winds whip through the terrain like a tornado, making the inferno so much worse.

The grounds were evacuated except for a group of people who remained to fight the fire. At about two-thirty in the afternoon, they prayed earnestly that God would turn the ninety-mile-per-hour winds away from the buildings. In another location, Vonette and I also got on our knees and began to pray that God would turn the winds.

The heat and smoke became so intense that those who were spraying water on the buildings were forced to lie on the ground to breathe. At two-thirty, they were at the point of abandoning our bungalow to the flames surrounding it on three sides. Then one of the firefighters observed the flag snapping violently in the wind. Suddenly, the flag began to turn, and within a few moments, it was flapping in the opposite direction. The winds had miraculously shifted and swept the flames in another direction. Our bungalow and other buildings were saved! All those who were fighting the fire were awestruck at what God had done before their very eyes! Yes, prayer truly changes things when we pray in faith!

Jesus commands us to forgive others before we pray. Jesus taught His disciples, "But when you are praying, first forgive anyone you are holding a grudge against, so that your Father in heaven will forgive your sins, too" (Mark 11:25). God wants us to pray with a pure heart, and He knows that a heart that harbors grudges is not ready to pray and see results.

We have no right to be unforgiving to someone else and then expect God to listen to us with no hesitation. Jesus gave up everything and suffered horribly to save us from our sins. For His sake, God has forgiven us of so much. How many sins do you think you have committed in your lifetime? Include all the sins of attitude as well as actions. We could never count them all. Then who do we think we are to hold a grudge against someone who has hurt us?

I have found this principle to be true in my own life. If I am aware of something I am holding against another person, my prayer life suffers. I don't feel the same freedom to go before the throne of God, and my prayers don't receive answers. I just imagine how Jesus must be viewing my actions when I hold back forgiveness for another but want Him to forgive me. Therefore, during my prayer times, I search my heart to see if I need to take care of an unforgiving spirit. If I find something, I realize that I must reconcile with the person against whom I am holding a grudge before I can expect God to hear my prayers.

HOW SHOULD WE PRAY?

Jesus was interested in prayer and modeled a rich prayer life for us. Because I want to follow His example and have effective communication with God, I make prayer a priority in my life. There is a sense in which I pray without ceasing, talking to God hundreds of times a day about everything. I begin my day in prayer, worshipping, praising, and adoring our great and gracious Creator God. I acknowledge Jesus as my Lord and Master. By faith, as an act of my will, I invite the Holy Spirit to control my life. I pray for wisdom about the numerous decisions I must make for that day. I pray for the salvation of friends and strangers. I pray for the healing of the sick and the spiritual and material needs of the Campus Crusade for Christ ministry. I also pray for the needs of my family, various staff members, and leaders of other Christian organizations. I pray for our national, state, and local leaders. I even pray about small personal matters that are of concern to me alone. And God answers!

I then like to spend time reading and meditating on God's Word. I often open the Bible and talk with God. I ask the Holy Spirit to make my reading meaningful to me. (For more about how to make Scripture reading meaningful, see *Discover the Book God Wrote*.)

As I read, I thank God for His loving salvation and provision, confessing any sins that the Scripture may reveal in my life. I ask God for the boldness and faith His apostles displayed, and I thank Him for the insights into His divine strategy of reaching the world with the good news of His love and forgiveness through Jesus our Lord. I often pause to pray about some special truth or claim a biblical promise.

In the evening, I once again worship the Lord, read His Word, and ask Him, "Lord, is there anything in me that is displeasing to You, anything I need to confess?" If the Holy Spirit reveals sins or weaknesses, I confess them and claim by faith God's victory for my life. Then I can know that since my last conscious thoughts are of Him, my subconscious thoughts will continue to worship Him all night long. When I waken, my first thoughts will be of our dear Lord.

I also spend time in prayer with Vonette, friends, and ministry partners. These are special times as we claim the promises of Jesus in prayer. I wish you could join us in these wonderful moments as we focus on God together!

Remember, as we bow in prayer, we are tapping into a source of power that can change the course of history. God's mighty power, His love, His wisdom, and His grace are available to us if we believe Him and claim them. Remember always, Jesus promised that we will do the same miracles He did, and even greater ones (see John 14:12). Prayer is the power behind our victory.

So far, we have learned about many areas in which Jesus modeled the life we should live and gave us principles that help us obey God. He expects us to respond to Him through Spirit-filled living by loving others and serving them and obeying the Father.

But one of Jesus' commands has been the focus of my life for fifty years: reaching the world with the love of Jesus. In our next section, we will discover the joy of spreading His love to others.

Read about the Real Jesus: Read one of Jesus' teachings about prayer:

> Keep on asking, and you will be given what you ask for. Keep on looking, and you will find. Keep on knocking, and the door will be opened. For everyone who asks, receives. Everyone who seeks, finds. And the door is opened to everyone who knocks. You parents—if your children ask for a loaf of bread, do you give them a stone instead? Or if they ask for a fish, do you give them a snake? Of course not! If you sinful people know how to give good gifts to your children, how much more will your heavenly Father give good gifts to those who ask Him.
>
> MATTHEW 7:7-11

1. Before you read this chapter, what did you think about prayer?

2. How have your ideas about prayer changed since you read about Jesus' example of prayer?

3. Describe what your prayer life is like.

4. How do the verses from Matthew 7 give you confidence about coming to God in prayer?

5. What will you do to change your prayer habits, to make them more in line with what Jesus expects of His followers?

PART 4

How Do I Spread My Love for Jesus?

~

Go and make disciples of all the nations, baptizing
them in the name of the Father and the Son and
the Holy Spirit. Teach these new disciples to
obey all the commands I have given you.

JESUS

14

The Body of Christ

*I*n recent years, I have suffered from a lung disease that has impaired my ability to breathe. I have also been afflicted with the aches and pains that go along with getting older. The Lord has blessed me with eight decades of life, and I thank Him for each year. They have been glorious opportunities to serve my Lord and enjoy the company of my wonderful wife, my two sons, and their families.

Years ago, as most young people do, I took my health more for granted than I do now. I was able to travel thousands of miles per year, speak hundreds of times, participate in countless important meetings, and enjoy so many other activities. I didn't realize then just how marvelous the simple act of breathing is.

Our bodies are remarkable. When we think about how many organs and systems our bodies have and how smoothly they all work together, we're astounded. Muscles and bones, blood vessels and the heart, nerves, intestines, liver—and so much more. The organ that has fascinated scientists the most is the brain. Researchers estimate that the brain has one hundred billion neurons, which are places where the brain receives information. Each of these neurons has at least eight different types of receptors. The neurons receive electrochemical signals at a speed of thousandths of a second. These communications control all the parts of our bodies.[1]

Think of how complex and unified the body is! Every part, including the brain, works together to accomplish whatever you want and need to do. Consider a simple activity like walking up a set of stairs. Your muscles, nerves, heart, lungs, eyes, and brain all coordinate to enable you to move with just the right balance and effort. Only God could have created something so intricate and highly functional.

The Bible tells us that the interrelatedness of the various parts of our bodies helps us understand Christ's body, the worldwide church—those people who truly believe that Jesus died for their sins and are children of God. "The human body has many parts, but the many parts make up only one body. So it is with the body of Christ. Some of us are Jews, some are Gentiles, some are slaves, and some are free. But we have all been baptized into Christ's body by one Spirit, and we have all received the same Spirit. Yes, the body has many different parts, not just one part" (1 Corinthians 12:12-14).

THE HEAD OF THE BODY

In what part of your body is the organ that controls the rest of the organs and systems? Your head, of course. Those billions of neurons in your brain are perfectly tuned to enable you to move, talk, sleep, and do any kind of activity. No one wakes up in the morning and says, "I think I'll let my liver call the shots today." We all realize that the only organ with the capacity to control us is our brain.

Here's how the apostle Paul explains Christ's role in the church: "We will hold to the truth in love, becoming more and more in every way like Christ, who is the head of His body, the church. Under His direction, the whole body is fitted together perfectly" (Ephesians 4:15-16).

This is the picture the Bible gives us. We, as the body of Christ, are all connected to each other. We are also placed in the body under the head— the control—of Jesus Christ. Everything we are is a result of Him. Paul explains, "We are joined together in His body by His strong sinews, and we grow only as we get our nourishment and strength from God" (Colossians 2:19).

What do you have that you did not receive from Jesus? He created you, gave you physical life. He made it possible for you to have spiritual life. He has provided everything in your world to sustain your life. Paul is telling us that Jesus also gives us the sustenance for our spiritual growth.

Let's go back to the example of walking up a set of stairs. The entire body must be coordinated in its effort to make it from the bottom step to the top one. The leg and arm muscles must act at just the right time. The heart and lungs must provide extra oxygen to the muscles. The eyes must look ahead. What would happen if one leg chose to boycott the activity? What if the lungs decided they didn't want to make the extra effort? Sounds ridiculous, doesn't it? The parts of the body must work together. Each part is unique and valuable.

That's also true of the body of Christ: "Just as our bodies have many parts and each part has a special function, so it is with Christ's body. We are all parts of His one body, and each of us has different work to do. And since we are all one body in Christ, we belong to each other, and each of us needs all the others" (Romans 12:4-5).

Just as an eye is not less valuable than the stomach or an ear less important than a kidney, each Christian in the body of Christ is precious. Paul explains,

> In fact, some of the parts that seem weakest and least important are really the most necessary. And the parts we regard as less honorable are those we clothe with the greatest care. So we carefully protect from the eyes of others those parts that should not be seen, while other parts do not require this special care. So God has put the body together in such a way that extra honor and care are given to those parts that have less dignity. This makes for harmony among the members, so that all the members care for each other equally. If one part suffers, all the parts suffer with it, and if one part is honored, all the parts are glad. Now all of you together are Christ's body, and each one of you is a separate and necessary part of it.
> (1 Corinthians 12:22-27)

The small child who lives in poverty in Africa is just as important to Jesus as the head of a Christian organization in America. The person who is a paraplegic has the same standing as an Olympic medalist. The elderly person suffering from Alzheimer's disease is loved by Jesus as much as the Yale graduate with a promising career. We are all part of Christ's body.

When did the church—the body of Christ—begin? At a spectacular moment when Jesus gave His last words on earth. From that time forward the world was forever changed.

THE BEGINNINGS OF THE CHURCH

After Christ's resurrection, He appeared to His disciples, called apostles at that point. Their hopes had plummeted into the depths of despair at the Crucifixion, but after the Resurrection, their faith in Jesus was even stronger. But they still didn't understand Jesus' role. They were expecting Him to throw the Roman army out of Jerusalem and the Jewish religious leaders out of the Temple, and set up His own kingdom. And they were going to help Him rule! After all, if Jesus had the power to come back from the dead, He could do anything!

How shortsighted the disciples were. Jesus could see all of history, and His heart ached for people all over the world, not just those in Jerusalem or Rome. He had a plan that would change the entire world.

This is what Jesus told the apostles, "When the Holy Spirit has come upon you, you will receive power and will tell people about Me everywhere—in Jerusalem, throughout Judea, in Samaria, and to the ends of the earth" (Acts 1:8). In these few words, Jesus gave the church its mission. He gives us the same mission today:

- *Go to Jerusalem*—which represents the city where you live and the people you know best.
- *Go to Judea*—which represents the people in your general area, people who live and speak as you do.
- *Go to Samaria*—which represents the people of different cultures and languages, people who live in places you are not familiar with.
- *Go to the ends of the earth*—which represents people in the most obscure places.

Telling people everywhere about Jesus is the church's main task today. All Christians are charged with the responsibility to tell others not only about Christ's love and forgiveness but also about the eternal life available to them if they accept Christ's atoning death.

Right after Jesus commissioned His apostles, something spectacular happened. Jesus was taken up into the sky and disappeared into a cloud. The apostles stared up, astounded. Then two angels appeared beside the apostles and said, "Men of Galilee, why are you standing here staring at the sky? Jesus has been taken away from you into heaven. And someday, just as you saw Him go, He will return!" (Acts 1:11).

Imagine what the apostles must have thought. They had seen and experienced so much with Jesus. What next?

They walked the half mile to Jerusalem and went to an upper room where other followers of Jesus were waiting. Jesus had told them, "Do not leave Jerusalem until the Father sends you what He promised. Remember, I have told you about this before. John baptized with water, but in just a few days you will be baptized with the Holy Spirit" (Acts 1:4-5). So the apostles obeyed. They waited, praying with a large group of other believers.

Fifty days after Jesus' resurrection the believers were all together in one room again when a huge noise like the sound of a windstorm filled the house. Tongues of fire appeared in the air and settled on the shoulders of all who were present. Then everyone began speaking in languages that they had never spoken before! They were all filled with the Holy Spirit (see Acts 2:1-4).

This is when the church, the body of Christ, was born. And what a beginning it was! The Holy Spirit had knit them all into one body.

Outside the house, people heard the strange noise of the wind, and they ran to see what was happening. Because the Jewish festival of Pentecost was being celebrated in Jerusalem, Jews from many places had come to the city. Many spoke different languages. But suddenly they were hearing the news about Jesus proclaimed in their own tongues!

They couldn't believe these Jewish believers could speak their languages.

"How can this be?" they exclaimed. "These people are all from Galilee, and yet we hear them speaking the languages of the lands where we were born! Here we are—Parthians, Medes, Elamites, people from Mesopotamia, Judea, Cappadocia, Pontus, the province of Asia, Phrygia, Pamphylia, Egypt, and the areas of Libya toward Cyrene, visitors from Rome (both Jews and converts to Judaism), Cretans, and Arabians. And we all hear these people speaking in our own languages about the wonderful things God has done!" They stood there amazed and perplexed. "What can this mean?" they asked each other. (Acts 2:7-12)

Isn't that just like Jesus? The first miracle His body, the church, performs is to spread the news about Him to the people in Jerusalem. And many of those who heard would take the news back to their homes, which were far away. Already the church was obeying Christ's commission.

This is what the Book of Acts says about those first few days of the church and the witness of the apostles. "Those who believed what Peter said were baptized and added to the church—about three thousand in all. They joined with the other believers and devoted themselves to the apostles' teaching and fellowship, sharing in the Lord's Supper and in prayer" (Acts 2:41-42). Those were exciting days!

JESUS AND THE CHURCH

Before Randy Johnson went to bed one Friday night, his dad gave him a chore to do the next morning. Several sprinkler heads in the yard needed to be fixed. Mr. Johnson took Randy out to the garage and selected the pipe fittings, sprinkler heads, pipe glue, and spades that Randy would need. Then the two of them went out to the yard. Randy's dad patiently explained exactly what he wanted his son to do. Randy asked a few questions, and his dad wrote down a few instructions on a piece of paper.

It took Randy several hours the next day to finish the job. But he worked carefully. When his dad came home, Randy took him out to the yard and showed him his work. Randy turned on the sprinklers; they ran perfectly. Mr. Johnson hugged his son. "You did a great job!" he said. "Let's celebrate by going to look for that video game you've been wanting for a long time."

Randy's dad was a good father. He provided not only the tools that Randy needed to do the job but also clear instructions for accomplishing the task. He showed Randy how much he appreciated his son and rewarded him for his good work.

This is similar to how Jesus takes care of His church. First, Jesus loves His church. Ephesians 5:29-30 says, "No one hates his own body but lovingly cares for it, just as Christ cares for His body, which is the church. And we are His body."

How much time per day do you spend caring for your body? You care for your body by eating, sleeping, showering, dressing, and exercising. And if one part of your body is injured, how much attention do you give it? Even if you just stub a toe, you stop and take care of that hurting part of your body.

Jesus cares for His church in similar ways. He tenderly treats our hurts and burdens. We could have no greater head than the One who loves us so much that He died for us.

The apostle Paul writes that Jesus loves us so much that He makes us clean and holy (see Ephesians 5:25-27). This process is called *sanctification*.

Jesus nurtures us the way a parent cares for a child, the way a godly husband cares for his wife. Christ wants us to grow and mature in our faith until we resemble Him more and more. This is how God the Father has set up this relationship for our sanctification: "God has put all things under the authority of Christ, and He gave Him this authority for the benefit of the church. And the church is His body; it is filled by Christ, who fills everything everywhere with His presence" (Ephesians 1:22-23).

But just as Mr. Johnson gave Randy the right tools and supplies to complete the sprinkler job, Jesus gives His body what it needs to complete its mission. Each of us receives gifts that enable us to accomplish the special tasks that He gives us to do. "We are all one body.... However, He has given each one of us a special gift according to the generosity of Christ" (Ephesians 4:4, 7). These spiritual gifts—teaching, preaching, giving in faith—help us mature in Christ and accomplish the mission. These gifts are to be used to help other members of the body and to help reach the world for Christ.

AMBASSADORS FOR CHRIST

How are you representing Jesus to the world? Are you using the talents, treasures, and time He has given you to reach out in love to others? The New Testament calls us ambassadors for Jesus (see 2 Corinthians 5:20). Just what do ambassadors do? They travel to foreign countries and represent the leader of their homeland. They attend events and make decisions in the name of their leader. They do things that the leader would do if he or she were in the foreign country. When we are Christ's ambassadors, whether in our own communities or in other places around the world, we represent Him. We become His presence—His body—wherever we go.

Sometimes representing Christ is like a battle. We are fighting unseen evil forces that don't want us to succeed. But as the representatives of Jesus, with Him always by our side, our victory is assured. We will always have what we need to tell others about Him.

Jeff Streucker was one of the elite army Rangers caught in the fighting in Mogadishu, Somalia, which was portrayed in the movie *Black Hawk Down*. A Christian, Jeff was twenty-four years old and in charge of nine men. His adventure began when his Humvee rescued an American who had fallen seventy feet from a helicopter. On the way back to the airfield, the unit faced gunfire from every side. One of Jeff's men was shot in the forehead and died before they could get back.

When Jeff's unit reached the airfield, his platoon leader ordered them back into the fighting to help rescue soldiers from a downed helicopter. When Jeff heard the orders, he believed he would likely die on his mission. He prayed, "God, I need Your help." Then he pictured Jesus on that night in the garden of Gethsemane when He prayed, "not My will, but Yours be done" (Luke 22:42, NIV).

Jeff prayed that same prayer for himself, feeling confident that God would take care of him. He believed that no matter what happened, if he lived or died, he would spend eternity with Jesus.

His resolve helped other members of his unit prepare themselves for the dangers ahead. Jeff says, "I did everything I could to tell as many soldiers as would listen about what would happen to them if they died—if they knew Jesus, they'd be fine."

Jeff cleaned the blood from his vehicle, and the soldiers made three more trips that night. Jeff made it through to reunite with his pregnant wife back home.[2]

No matter what God calls us to do, Jesus goes before us with His love, strength, and wisdom. He gives us gifts to accomplish His will. As part of His body, we can be sure that every one of us is an essential part of His worldwide plan!

THE GREAT COMMISSION OF JESUS

The mission that Jesus gave the church is often called the Great Commission: "I have been given complete authority in heaven and on earth. Therefore, go and make disciples of all the nations, baptizing them in the name of the Father and the Son and the Holy Spirit. Teach these new disciples to obey all the commands I have given you. And be sure of this: I am with you always, even to the end of the age" (Matthew 28:18-20).

This is the greatest and most fulfilling task ever given to anyone. And we can have a part! In the next chapter, I want to show you just how wonderful and exciting it is to be part of the worldwide mission that Jesus has given us!

Discover Jesus

Read about the Real Jesus: Jesus gave us the following command:

> When the Holy Spirit has come upon you, you will receive
> power and will tell people about Me everywhere—in Jerusalem,
> throughout Judea, in Samaria, and to the ends of the earth.
>
> ACTS 1:8

1. How do you think the followers of Jesus felt about this command after Jesus had gone back to heaven?

2. When you hear this command, does it make you feel excited, threatened, worried, or confused?

3. How do you think Jesus wants you to participate in spreading the news about His love for people?

4. What kinds of gifts do you think Jesus has given you to enable you to do this?

5. How do you feel about being part of such a wonderful company as the body of Christ?

15

The Mission of Jesus

*N*early seventy years ago, a young man turned his life over to Christ and began earnestly bringing the message of Jesus to others. Within months of his decision to follow the Lord Jesus, he was discipling other young people. Before long, the young man had gathered a small number of Christian friends, and together they went to the hills of California to pray. They prayed for each other, but the focus of their prayers was their country and the world as they pleaded with God for the salvation of people everywhere. Those heartfelt prayers led to the founding of the Navigators, which grew into a worldwide ministry that has led multitudes of men and women to Christ. The young man's name was Dawson Trotman.

I remember Dawson as an ambitious man. He was one of the first people I met when I moved to Los Angeles. But unlike some of the great moguls and financial wizards of our time, Dawson was motivated by godly ambition. This led him to accomplish extraordinary things for the Lord Jesus Christ rather than for himself. His vision and enthusiasm strongly influenced my own desire to build disciples who would help fulfill the Great Commission of Jesus.

From 1951, when Campus Crusade for Christ was founded, until now, the unquestionable call on my life is to help fulfill the Great Commission. From the time I awaken every morning until I go to bed every night, I evaluate everything I do in the light of the Great Commission. I undertake every appointment, every trip, every message so that I will help reach the largest number of people with the gospel.

I remember that first year of our ministry at UCLA. We put a map of the world in front of us. Although the ministry included only a handful of us, even then we believed that God would reach the entire world with the message of Jesus. That was the vision God gave us—to help reach the world for Christ. I emphasize the word *help* because we are only a part of the great body of Christ. But we are seeing the most unprecedented spiritual harvest in the history of the world. From the beginning of our organization we have tried to evaluate everything we do according to how it fits into the Great Commission.

A recent example is the tragedy that happened on September 11, 2001. At the time, we had a hundred staff members serving in the New York City area, but they couldn't handle the tremendous need that people had at that time. Chuck Price, the U.S. director of Campus Crusade, set up a temporary assignment opportunity for other staff members to travel to New York as part of a rescue effort. Throughout that next year, 240 staff members came to New York. They found that people all over the city were questioning the purpose of life and why this tragedy had happened. One staff member spoke to high school students who had seen the Twin Towers collapse from their school's window. All over the great city, people were open to hear about the claims of Jesus.

As part of our effort to address the needs of people we met, we arranged for the printing of a minimagazine called *Fallen but Not Forgotten*. Within the year, the magazine had been translated into four different languages, and more than 11 million copies were distributed across the United States. In the midst of the dust of the collapsed Twin Towers, many people found peace in the Lord. People were incredibly eager to hear about Jesus.[1]

SPIRITUAL MULTIPLICATION

"This is all well and good," you may be saying to yourself, "but I don't live in an area that is dealing with such a horrific tragedy. And how could I reach so many people with the gospel? Jesus' command to reach the whole world just sounds impossible! Do you know how many people that is?"

What's amazing about the plan that Jesus gave us is that it is doable! That's because of a spiritual principle that I like to call *spiritual multiplication*.

We all know that growth by multiplication is much more effective than growth by addition. Do you have a savings plan? Consider two different methods of saving. In Plan A, you put $100 into your bank account every day for a month. Your account would grow pretty fast. But in Plan B, you put a penny into your savings on the first day, then you double your savings by putting in two cents the next day. You continue to double the input for the whole month. Which of the two plans do you think will accumulate more money? If you chose Plan B, you were right. Plan A would accumulate $3,000 by the end of the month, but Plan B results in $10,737,418.23! Multiplication always leads to rapid growth.

The multiplication principle is why discipling others in how to share the message of Jesus with others is so important to the spread of God's Kingdom. In fact, consider this possibility: A Christian leads only one person to Christ each year, but he or she spends the rest of the year discipling that new believer. By the end of the year, both the original Christian and the convert lead someone else to Christ. Now there are four Christians. Then the process starts all over again. If this simple process continues for twenty-five years, the result would be more than 33 million new Christians! Theoretically, through spiritual multiplication the world's population could be reached in less than thirty-four years! So you can see what an effect your obedience to the command of Jesus can have in your community, your state, and even our country.

A little over twenty years ago, a man named Boonma was our director in Thailand. He was an amazing example of spiritual multiplication. He and his wife, Chalong, received their training at our Great Commission Training Center in the Philippines in 1980. They returned to Thailand, and within six years, they trained 700 people to share their faith and teach others to do the same. In turn, these disciples have trained 90,000 people who are now involved in winning and discipling still others.

One person Boonma trained led more than 10,000 people to Christ using a flip chart featuring an amplified version of the gospel. Many of those he introduced to Christ are today helping to start New Life Bible study groups in thousands of homes and establishing hundreds of churches. This is only one example of what can be done through the principle of spiritual multiplication.

Over the years, Campus Crusade for Christ has grown from a staff of two—Vonette and me on the campus of UCLA—to 26,000 full-time staff and 225,000 trained volunteers in 191 countries. Tens of millions around the world have received Christ, and many of these have discipled others to do the same as a result of this ministry.

Sometimes people ask me, "Are you surprised at the phenomenal growth and success of Campus Crusade?"

My answer is, "No!" God is in the business of spiritual multiplication, and according to the original vision He gave us in 1951 to help reach the world for Christ, we have only begun to see what He is going to do!

THE IMPORTANCE OF WITNESSING

Perhaps right now you are thinking that you could never get excited about sharing your faith with others. Maybe you've thought that witnessing about Jesus is just not for you.

I once met a man who told me, "I don't wear my religion on my sleeve. My religion is personal and private. I don't want to talk about it."

The man who made this statement was one of America's leading statesmen and a professing Christian. He was the guest speaker at a meeting near the campus of Harvard University. I had just asked him to get involved, along with a thousand key Christian leaders, in a worldwide effort to help fulfill the Great Commission. His statement startled me.

I asked him, "You're a Christian, aren't you?"

"Yes, but I'm not a religious fanatic."

Grieved by his logic, I continued to prod him gently. "Did it ever occur to you that it cost Jesus Christ His life so that you could call yourself a Christian? It cost the disciples their lives too, and millions of Christians throughout the centuries have suffered or died as martyrs to get the message of God's love and forgiveness to you. Do you really believe that your faith in Christ is personal and private and that you shouldn't talk about it?"

He thought for a moment, then conceded, "No sir, I'm wrong. Tell me what I can do about it."

During fifty years of sharing Christ and training others to do the same, I've found no biblical rationale to justify keeping silent. In fact, the need for people to hear the good news about Jesus' sacrifice for us is a matter of life and death. The writer of Ecclesiastes observes, "You are going to die, and you should think about it while there is still time" (7:2).

The night after September 11, 2001, Chuck Price attended a meeting in the offices of our marketplace ministry, Priority Associates. Eighty people were present to talk about their grief and to hear a presentation of the gospel.

After Chuck addressed the group, a young man came up to him, put his head on Chuck's shoulders, and began to weep. As the young man cried, he told his story. He had been near the Twin Towers when the airplanes crashed into them. He had seen several people leap out of the buildings to their deaths before the towers collapsed.

The young man kept repeating, "I worked with those people every day, and I never talked to them about the Lord, and I'll never have an opportunity again to talk to those people."[2]

Most of us will never face a crisis as dire as that young man's, but all around us are people who need Jesus' love just as desperately. The elderly man who is facing death without knowing for sure where he's going. The young mother who just found out that her unfaithful husband is leaving her and now must find a way to raise her three children alone. The young college student who is caught up in a trap of Internet pornography and doesn't know how to get out. The wealthy relative who has everything but feels empty inside. The neighbor who has just been diagnosed with pancreatic cancer. You can bring hope to people like this. You can tell them about Jesus' love for them and about the heaven He has prepared for those who believe. That's why witnessing is the most important thing you can do as a believer.

EIGHT REASONS TO WITNESS

Jesus placed such a high value on the human soul that He gladly exchanged the perfection of heaven for a lifetime of poverty, suffering, shame, and death to seek and save those who were lost without God's love (see Luke 19:10). From His earliest youth and throughout His life, Jesus clearly understood His mission and purpose. His concern for the lost was so deep that at times the flood of compassionate tears rolled down His face. Jesus, the manliest of men, wept. All because He saw the human plight without God.

In the Great Commission, our Lord gave us the greatest mission in history. He said, "Go and make disciples." It is our deepest calling to share His love and forgiveness with those who have never received Him as their Savior and Lord.

From my personal experiences and through the study of God's Word, I have discovered eight key concepts about witnessing. They will encourage us to be open with others about what Jesus has done for us.

1. Christ Gave the Command to Every Christian

The Great Commission was not introduced merely for the eleven remaining disciples, for the apostles, or for those who may have the gift of evangelism today. This command is the responsibility of every man and woman who professes faith in Christ.

I was recently talking to a staff friend who had been to a showroom where the latest models in reclining chairs were displayed. He tried one that massages your neck, back, and legs, provides heat, and even has a built-in stereo. It cost $2,000. My friend commented, "It was so comfortable that I was tempted never to get up again."

That's how many Christians approach their spiritual life. They live comfortably as if they were sitting in such a chair—relaxed and insulated from God's command in the Great Commission. After all, life is comfortable for them because they have the joy of fellowship with God and other Christians.

When Christ commanded us to go into all the world, He did not call us to kick back in an easy chair. Spreading the gospel will not happen by remote control—only by disciples willing to stand up and "go."

2. All Men and Women Are Lost without Jesus

Today, it is fashionable to say, "There are many ways to get to God—Confucianism, Mormonism, Hinduism, Scientology, New Age philosophy, and more." But God's Word tells us about Jesus, "There is salvation in no one else! There is no other name in all of heaven for people to call on to save them" (Acts 4:12).

Do you remember the lostness that you felt before you met Jesus? He is the only bridge between sinful mankind and a holy God. Without Him, people cannot know God, and they have no hope of eternal life. Men without Christ are eternally lost! Women without Christ are eternally lost! Families without Christ are empty and meaningless. Without Jesus, we can't find purpose in life.

One reason we tell men and women about Jesus is so they can experience a life overflowing with joy, blessing, and purpose. But unless we tell them, how will they know the abundant life Jesus promises?

3. People of the World Are Hungry to Know Jesus

One of the most prevalent misconceptions held by Christians today is that men and women don't want to know Jesus. But wherever I go around the world and in our country, I find ample proof that just the opposite is true. The Holy Spirit has created a hunger for God in the hearts of millions!

I have discovered that at least 25 to 50 percent of nonbelievers are ready to receive Christ in most parts of the world if they are properly approached, one on one, by a Spirit-empowered witness. And I believe that among that number may be some of your own family members, a neighbor or coworker, or a stranger to whom God will lead you. These people are ready to hear a clear and simple presentation of the good news of God's love and forgiveness.

Can we afford to be selfish with the gospel when such overwhelming evidence shows that so many people are hungry for God? By sharing our faith in Christ with others, we can help change our world for our Lord.

4. We Have in Our Possession God's Gift of Eternal Life

Fritz Kreisler, the world-famous violinist, earned a fortune with his concerts and compositions, but he generously gave most of it away. One day on one of his trips he discovered an exquisite violin, but he didn't have the money to buy it. Later, having raised enough to meet the asking price, he returned to the seller, hoping to purchase that beautiful instrument. To his dismay, it had been sold to a collector.

Kreisler made his way to the collector's home and offered to buy the violin. The new owner said it was his prized possession, so he would not sell it. Keenly disappointed, Kreisler was about to leave when he had an idea. "Could I play the instrument once more before it is consigned to silence?"

The owner granted permission, and the great virtuoso filled the room with such heart-moving music that the collector's emotions were deeply stirred. "I have no right to keep that to myself," he exclaimed. "It's yours, Mr. Kreisler. Take it into the world, and let people hear it."[3]

We have the most precious gift the world could ever know. Christ is risen! We serve a living Savior! He not only lives within us in all His resurrection power but also assures us of eternal life. Because He died in our place, we have direct fellowship with God. And this relationship, this peace, this gift of eternal life is available to all who receive Him. We have no right to keep this gift to ourselves.

5. Our Love for Jesus Compels Us to Share Him with Others

Jesus said, "Those who obey My commandments are the ones who love Me. And because they love Me, My Father will love them, and I will love them.

And I will reveal Myself to each one of them" (John 14:21). In other words, Jesus measures our love for Him by the extent and genuineness of our obedience to Him. As we obey, He promises He will reveal Himself to us.

When I think of how much Jesus has done for me, I can do no less than serve Him by sharing Him with others. He has done more for me than anyone else ever could. It humbles me to think that He calls me His friend and brother. How can I hide this great love from the eyes of other people?

I reaffirm what the apostle Paul wrote, "Everywhere we go, we tell everyone about Christ" (Colossians 1:28). My witness to others is this: Jesus loves me so much that I want to tell you about Him because He loves you just as much as He loves me. Over the years, as I have obeyed His command to tell others, Jesus has shown me time and again the depth of His love for them. As I have seen His love for others, I have also recognized the depth of His love for me!

6. God Offers Great Benefits to Those Who Receive Christ

Of all the exciting privileges that God has given me through the years, none compares with that of introducing others to Jesus. It is humbling to know that God has allowed me the incredible joy of introducing many thousands to Him through individual conversations and meetings, large and small. When I consider the benefits that come to those who receive Christ, I sometimes wonder how anyone could ever say no to Jesus. The benefits to those who receive Christ include the following:

- They become children of God.
- Their bodies become temples of God.
- They receive forgiveness for all of their sins.
- They begin to experience the peace and love of God.
- They receive God's direction and purpose for their lives.
- They experience the power of God to change their lives.
- They have assurance of eternal life.

One of my greatest joys is explaining these benefits to those who have just become children of God.

7. Obedience to the Great Commission Is a Privilege

Rusty Stephens, who works with the Navigators, tells a story of how mowing the grass with his young son taught him about how God sees us when we try to help Him share the Good News. "As I feverishly pushed the lawn mower around our yard, I wondered if I'd finish before dinner. Mikey, our six-year-old, walked up, stepped in front of me, and placed his hands on the mower handle. Knowing that he wanted to help me, I quit pushing. The mower quickly slowed to a stop. Chuckling inwardly at his struggles, I resisted the urge to say, 'Get out of here, kid. You're in my way.' Instead I said, 'Here, son, I'll help you.' As I continued pushing, I bowed my back, leaned forward, and walked spread-legged to avoid colliding with my son. I continued to mow, but the process was much slower and less efficient because Mikey was 'helping' me.

"Suddenly, tears came to my eyes. I realized that this is the way God allows me the honor to 'help' Him build His Kingdom! I pictured my heavenly Father at work seeking, saving, and transforming the lost, and there I was, with my weak hands, 'helping.' God could do the work by Himself, but He doesn't. He chooses to stoop graciously to allow me, His son, to colabor with Him. Why? For my sake, because He wants me to experience the joy and privilege of ministering with Him."[4]

It has been my privilege to meet and fellowship with some of the most famous, powerful, wealthy, influential people in the world: kings, presidents, and leaders in business and industry. On many occasions, I have had my picture taken, sometimes at my request, with some of the world's most distinguished people.

But of all the privileges of life and all the honors that have come to me, none even begins to compare with the unspeakable privilege that God has given me to act as His ambassador to the world. To share the glorious, gracious, incomparable Savior with others is an honor beyond words. It is one of the greatest blessings of my life. It can be yours as well.

8. Witnessing Is the Most Important Thing Believers Can Do

All over the world, I have asked two questions of believers, young and old, rich and poor, new believers and people who have followed Christ for more than half a century. I have asked these questions of some of the most famous Christians in the world. The answers are always the same, no matter whom I ask.

Question one: "What is the most important experience of your life?"
Answer: "Knowing Christ as my Savior."
Question two: "What is the most important thing you can do for another person?"

Answer: "Help him or her to know Jesus."

If you are a Christian, you undoubtedly would give the same answers to these questions. Witnessing is the most significant thing you can do for others. Commit yourself today to being filled and empowered with the Holy Spirit so that you will be an effective witness for Christ and His gospel. There is no greater or more thrilling adventure in life than to be Christ's ambassador.

If you want to experience a life of high adventure and deepest satisfaction, one that will result in eternal differences in the lives of your family, friends, and people you have not yet met, begin witnessing as a way of life. Look for every opportunity to introduce people to Jesus. Ask God to lead you to people who are hungry for His love. When you do, remember what happens in witnessing: *Success in witnessing is simply taking the initiative to share Christ in the power of the Holy Spirit and leaving the results to God!* If you obey, no matter what the results, you will please God. He is the One who changes hearts. He expects us just to be faithful to Christ's command to help fulfill the Great Commission.

If you would like to learn more about sharing your faith, you can find excellent resources in your local Christian bookstore. My book *Witnessing without Fear* will lead you through some basic principles and ways to share your faith with confidence. Campus Crusade also has seminars and other training methods to help you become more effective in sharing your faith. You can visit www.ccci.org to receive more information.

Without a doubt, sharing our love for Jesus gives us an exciting, fulfilling life. He is beside us, helping us, guiding us, loving us. As we will discover in the next chapter, He is the Savior who never fails us.

Read about the Real Jesus: What work did Jesus give to you?

> I have been given complete authority in heaven and on earth.
> Therefore, go and make disciples of all the nations, baptizing
> them in the name of the Father and the Son and the Holy Spirit.
> Teach these new disciples to obey all the commands I have given
> you. And be sure of this: I am with you always, even to the end
> of the age.
>
> MATTHEW 28:18-20

1. What feelings do you have when you think of witnessing for Jesus?

2. What does Jesus say in these verses to give you more confidence in sharing your faith?

3. How does it make you feel to know that Jesus will help you spread the gospel?

4. List some names of people that you would like to introduce to Jesus.

5. Pray, asking God to give you opportunities to tell these people about how much Jesus means to you.

16

A Savior Who Never Fails

*H*ave you ever done something that, if you had known the future, you would have done differently? Perhaps you began something that you didn't realize would be so full of responsibility but that eventually resulted in wonderful rewards. Certainly parenting fits into that category. If young couples could see all the hard times that come as a result of rearing children, they might never have children. New parents rarely envision themselves as the parents of a teenager! Yet the rewards of parenting children definitely outweigh all the difficulties. Becoming parents is a turning point that completely changes a couple's life.

One moment in Vonette's and my life served as such a turning point. It happened at a time when I acted very insensitively as a husband. One Sunday morning Vonette and I went to Hollywood Presbyterian Church to attend Sunday school and the church service. During Sunday school, I was called out to join a counseling session, so Vonette attended the meetings alone.

After the church service was over, she didn't know where I was, so she walked out to the parking lot to wait in our car. Soon everyone else left, and she still saw no sign of me. It must have seemed like an eternity to her as one hour passed, then a second one. Finally, during the third hour, I appeared.

I was a relatively new husband at that time, but I had no excuse for treating Vonette the way I did. She heatedly argued that I certainly would have felt hurt if our roles had been reversed and if she had left me sitting in a steaming parking lot for hours!

This whole incident brought up the subject of what we expected out of our relationship. After discussing our problems over lunch, we decided to write down our expectations. We each took sheets of paper to a separate room and prayed, asking God what He wanted us to accomplish in our marriage. When we finished, we met and shared our lists with each other.

Vonette, who has always been so practical, had written goals such as having children, a home nice enough to minister to people of all walks of life, a suitable car, and God's blessings. I took a more global approach. I wanted to place every detail of our lives under the control of our Lord Jesus Christ. The apostle Paul began several of his letters to believers by referring to himself as a slave of Jesus Christ. That's what I wanted to be too. In fact, I put on my list that I wanted to be Christ's slave.

I suggested to Vonette that we make our combined lists a "contract with God," a written statement that we wanted to surrender ourselves and everything we had totally and irrevocably to Him. Wherever He wanted us to go, we would go. Whatever He wanted us to do, we would do. Whatever it cost, we would be willing. We signed those papers and prayed, telling God what we were prepared to do. We gave our all to Him. The peace we felt was truly indescribable.

We made that decision fifty years ago. You may be wondering if we regret what we did. Absolutely not! I am still a slave of Jesus Christ. I claim no "rights." I do not feel I have ownership of Campus Crusade for Christ. I do not even own my life because I am not my own—I belong to Jesus. I have been bought with a price, the blood of Jesus. Because of Him, I have experienced the most abundant life I could ever have imagined.

Now, after all these years of knowing Jesus, I can speak with authority and conviction to agnostics and materialists. I tried their way of life. I experienced all it had to offer, and none of it compared with the life I have had in following Jesus. As I obeyed His commandments, I experienced the richest, most fulfilling, adventuresome life possible. Jesus said in Mark 8 that only those who put aside their own desires and follow Him could know what it means to really live. This is what I have done all these years—really lived.

People ask me, "When history looks back and sees what Bill Bright has accomplished for the Kingdom of God, what do you think others will say was your greatest contribution?"

I reply, "I do not know. I hope that people will say that he was faithful to a heavenly vision. That Bill Bright loved Jesus with all his heart. And that he was a man of faith, a man of courage willing to take risks for Jesus." Frankly, I do not know what people will say, but slaves do not need applause.

THE VISION

Not long after Vonette and I signed our contract, God gave me a vision for Campus Crusade for Christ. I believe that if we had not surrendered everything to Him, He would not have entrusted us with this call. Our attitudes of submission made us ready for His service.

The vision happened one night as I was studying for a Hebrew exam at Fuller Seminary. A friend was studying with me when suddenly God opened my mind and touched my heart. My experience that midnight hour was so rich, so meaningful, and yet so indescribable. People have asked me what happened. There is no way I can explain it. All I can say is that I met with God. I didn't see a physical form, I didn't hear an audible voice, but I have never been the same since that unforgettable encounter. The vision I received was to help reach the world for Christ and fulfill the Great Commission in my lifetime. I was to start on the college campuses, where future leaders were being trained. The slogan would be, "Reach the campus for Christ today—reach the world for Christ tomorrow."

God showed me that I was totally inadequate to accomplish this vision but that He was absolutely adequate. He wanted me to help Him, the Ruler of the universe! I had no idea how such an impossible task could be accomplished, but I knew that God did!

After the experience, which probably took only a few minutes, I felt ecstatic. I turned to my classmate, who had no idea what had happened to me, and suggested that we go for a midnight run. I was so full of energy and excitement, I just had to do something.

Early the next morning, I told Vonette about my vision, and she rejoiced with me. The more we prayed about what we were to do, the more excited she became. We decided to go into full-time Christian ministry. There was no turning back!

After we started Campus Crusade for Christ, we worked many, many hours. For years I traveled day and night. I was greatly motivated. The apostle Paul expressed what I felt: "Whatever we do, it is because Christ's love controls us [urges us on]" (2 Corinthians 5:14).

To me, serving the Lord has never been a job. It has been a privilege, a joy.

It is so exciting, not only because I have been liberated out of the darkness of Satan's kingdom, but also because I have had the privilege of being an ambassador for Christ as He seeks and saves the lost.

One of the most amazing truths about living for Jesus is that He is with us always (see Matthew 28:20). I have found that to be true in my life. Whenever I have needed Him, He has been there. When I was weak, He was my strength. When I was discouraged, He comforted me. I have failed Him many times, but He never once failed me![1]

JESUS IS FAITHFUL

It doesn't take spectacular talents or riches to earn the favor of Jesus. All He asks is that you surrender your heart—every nook and cranny of it—to Him. When you do, you will find just what I did—that you can have no better friend than Jesus. I could tell you hundreds of experiences that illustrate this biblical truth. But let me share four areas in which Jesus will do for you what He has done for me.

1. Jesus Never Fails Us in Times of Discouragement

When a person takes risks for Jesus, times of discouragement will inevitably come. As president of a worldwide mission organization, I waded through many of these moments. But Jesus was always there for me.

A number of years ago, my world seemed to be crumbling around me. All that I had worked for in the ministry of Campus Crusade for Christ was hanging by a slender thread—which was about to break. Because of a series of unforeseen circumstances, we were facing a financial crisis that could bankrupt the movement and result in the loss of our beautiful facilities at Arrowhead Springs, California, which then served as our international headquarters.

When the word came to me that everything we had planned and prayed for was almost certain to be lost, I fell to my knees and began to thank the Lord. Why would I thank God? Why would I do what some would consider a foolish act? Because many years before I had discovered that thanksgiving demonstrates faith, and without faith we cannot please God (see Hebrews 11:6).

As I was praising and thanking God in the midst of the crisis, His supernatural peace flooded my heart. I received the assurance that a miracle was on the way. In a few days, totally apart from my own abilities to solve the problem, God brought the right people into the right circumstances and performed a miracle. He provided the necessary finances to save Arrowhead Springs and the ministry.

I claim this promise from God during times of discouragement. You can too. "'I will never fail you. I will never forsake you.' That is why we can say with confidence, 'The Lord is my helper, so I will not be afraid'" (Hebrews 13:5-6).

2. Jesus Never Fails Us during Satan's Attacks

Because I grew up in a rural community on a ranch five miles from the nearest town, I received the first seven years of my education in a one-room, country school. I was often the only student in my class, and there were never more than three of us. It was not unusual for some big bully to pick on a student smaller than himself, and fights would start.

My dad taught me never to run from a fight because that was not the manly thing to do, so sometimes I found myself facing a fight with a bully. My brother, who was several years older, would stand by to insure that the fighting was fair and that someone would not take advantage of me.

The Lord Jesus Christ is like my older brother. He stands by to help us, to make us strong, and to guard us from the attacks of Satan, who is like the big bully.

Two thousand years ago, Satan was defeated at the Cross. He has no control over us except what God allows and what we by our disobedience and unbelief enable him to have. Why, then, do average Christians have such a tough time living the Christian life? Because they do not understand that the battle has already been won! Victory is ours. The apostle Paul writes, "The Lord is faithful; He will make you strong and guard you from the evil one" (2 Thessalonians 3:3). Nothing can touch us or harm us, whether we are criticized, persecuted, or even martyred for the sake of the kingdom. We are citizens of the heavenly kingdom. While we are here on this earth, Christ will surround us with His supernatural peace and power, turning tragedy into triumph, heartache and sorrow to joy. This is our heritage if only we keep on trusting and obeying Him.[2]

3. Jesus Never Fails Us during Times of Trial

No trial was greater than the one our ministry faced during the summer of 1976. Thirty-five female staff leaders, including Vonette, gathered for a Colorado retreat just before our entire staff training meetings began in Fort Collins in July. They were enjoying fellowship and training in the Big

Thompson Canyon when the rain began to pour. Soon, the women were in the midst of a flash flood.

I was awakened at about 1:30 in the morning and informed of the flood and of the rescue of one of the women, who was taken to the hospital. About an hour later, another staff member was brought to the hospital by helicopter. By this time, we had good reason to believe that several of the women at the retreat had drowned.

I didn't know if Vonette was safe, struggling for her life in the flood-waters, or dead. But I had an incredible peace because I knew that God is sovereign and ever-present. So even though I had no idea where Vonette was and could not help her, I trusted God was with her and the other women. Because He is all-powerful, He could save all the women whose lives were in danger. But God is also all-knowing. If He determined that Vonette would be taken home to heaven, I could completely trust my loving Savior to do the right thing.

Soon, we learned the sad news that seven of our staff women were among the victims who perished during the flood. I knew that each of these women was rejoicing in the presence of her Savior. I also learned that Vonette and twenty-seven other staff women had narrowly escaped the raging water.

In the weeks that followed, we mourned for those dear friends we had lost. But we also felt led to make their last moments of life a tribute to our sovereign God. With full approval of the grieving families, friends of Campus Crusade ministry placed full-page ads in most newspapers across the country, featuring pictures of the seven women who had died. The headline read, "These seven women lost their lives in the Colorado flood, but they are alive and they have a message for you." The rest of the ad gave readers an opportunity to read the gospel and receive Jesus Christ as their Savior. Approximately 150 million people read those ads. The response was phenomenal. Only God knows the full extent of what happened, but many thousands wrote to say that they had received Christ that week as a result of the tragic death of those seven women.

To this day, I thank God for the peace and confidence He provided through that experience. He proved to me beyond words that being His child is more than a superficial slogan about joy and blessing. Christ is the anchor of our souls—the only true source of life in all its fullness. Through our grief, we could claim the promise that "despite all these things, overwhelming victory is ours through Christ, who loved us" (Romans 8:37).

4. Jesus Never Fails Us through the Stages of Life

I don't know what stage of life you are in—whether you are a young adult, a parent, or a senior citizen. But you can have complete confidence that Jesus is beside you at this moment. Jesus promises, "No, I will not abandon you as orphans—I will come to you" (John 14:18).

At times in our lives, we all feel alone. Bev was a widow in her late seventies. Her family members were involved in their own careers and activities. Although they loved her, they were so busy that they seldom saw her to express that love. "I feel so alone," she said, "with my husband gone and all my children married. Sometimes I can hardly bear the pain, the anguish. At times it's as if I am about to suffocate, I am so lonely!"

I shared with her the good news of the One who loved her so much that He died on the cross for her and paid the penalty for her sins. I told her how He promised He would come to her and never leave her.

There in the loneliness of her living room, she bowed with me in prayer and invited the risen, living Christ to take up residence in her life. When she lifted her face, her cheeks were moist with tears of repentance and her heart was made new with joy.

"I feel so different," she said. "Already I feel enveloped with the sense of God's presence, love, and peace."

As the months passed, it became increasingly clear that she was not alone. He who was with her had been faithful to His promise never to leave her.

Do you feel deserted, alone, rejected? Do you have problems with your family, work, school, or health? Whatever your need or your place in life, Jesus is waiting to make His presence as real to you as if He were with you in His physical body. You are never alone.[3]

NOW IT'S YOUR TURN

We have spent many moments together in the pages of this book, exploring the life and character of Jesus. We have seen His love, sacrifice, compassion, and grace toward us. We have seen His tender heart and His wisdom.

Are you ready to be a slave of Jesus Christ? Do you feel enough confidence in Him to place your life and everything you own into His hands?

Jesus wants to have more than a casual relationship with you. He wants to be your best friend, your guide, your Lord. Whatever He has planned for the rest of your life will be the greatest pathway you could ever travel!

Jesus says, "If any of you wants to be My follower, you must put aside your selfish ambition, shoulder your cross, and follow Me. If you try to keep your life for yourself, you will lose it. But if you give up your life for Me, you will find true life" (Matthew 16:24-25). I have had the privilege of meeting so many believers who have given their all to Jesus: struggling students, successful businessmen and women, famous athletes, world leaders, stay-at-home moms, blue-collar workers, and retired saints. They all say the same thing. What God has planned for their lives fits them uniquely and fulfills them completely. Whatever they "lost" by following Jesus has turned out to be insignificant compared to what they gained in His presence. I have heard people from every corner of the world praise Jesus for providing them the abundant life—no matter what their circumstances may be.

In 1947 I was greatly affected by Scotland's Dr. James Stewart, one of the most famous New Testament scholars of his time. He said of Jesus: "If we could show the world that being committed to Christ is no tame, humdrum, sheltered monotony, but the most exciting, thrilling adventure the human spirit can ever know, those who have been standing outside the church and looking askance at Christ will come crowding in to pay allegiance, and we might well expect the greatest revival since Pentecost."[4]

Millions of people are discovering the importance of having an intimate relationship with Jesus. They are turning away from their "religions" to embrace the One who died for them. They are seeing that walking with Him is the most exhilarating life imaginable. What we do for Jesus will make all the difference in the world to us and to so many others we come in contact with every day. Since we have the eternal privilege of knowing and serving the greatest Person in history, our great God and Savior Jesus Christ, how can we do anything else?

Discover Jesus

Read about the Real Jesus: Read what Jesus told us about how we are to live our lives:

> If any of you wants to be My follower, you must put aside your selfish ambition, shoulder your cross, and follow Me. If you try to keep your life for yourself, you will lose it. But if you give up your life for Me, you will find true life.
>
> MATTHEW 16:24-25

1. What in your life comes between you and your total commitment to Jesus?

2. What does Jesus mean when He says that we will find true life only when we give up our life for Him?

3. How would your life change if you made this commitment to Jesus?

4. What do you think Jesus is talking about when He says you must "shoulder your cross"?

5. Commit yourself to be a slave of Jesus Christ, and thank Him for the privilege of serving Him and of receiving all that He has prepared for you.

NOTES

Chapter 1—A Momentous Decision

1. This story is also told in Michael Richardson's book *Amazing Faith: The Authorized Biography of Bill Bright* (Colorado Springs, Colo.: WaterBrook, 2000), 1–23.
2. Josh McDowell, *The New Evidence That Demands a Verdict,* rev. ed. (Nashville: Nelson, 1999), xxiv.

Chapter 2—"Who Do People Say That I Am?"

1. Charles Malik, *Christ and Crisis* (Grand Rapids: Eerdmans, 1962), 67–70.

Chapter 3—What Does Jesus Say about Himself?

1. C. S. Lewis, *Mere Christianity* (New York: Macmillan, 1960), 56.

Chapter 4—The Miraculous Birth

1. This chart and the following statistics are taken from Bill Bright, *A Man without Equal* (Orlando: NewLife Publications, 1992), 39–41.
2. Peter W. Stoner and Robert C. Newman, *Science Speaks: Scientific Proof of the Accuracy of Prophecy and the Bible* (Chicago: Moody Press, 1976), 40–41.

Chapter 5—The Mystery of Two in One

1. *Tyndale Bible Dictionary,* eds. Walter A. Elwell and Philip W. Comfort (Wheaton, Ill.: Tyndale, 2001), s.v. "Christology."
2. Ibid.
3. Bill Bright, *A Man without Equal* (Orlando: NewLife Publications, 1992), 49–50.

Chapter 6—Our Good Shepherd

1. This story is told in Robert Schuller's book *The Be (Happy) Attitudes: Eight Positive Attitudes That Can Transform Your Life* (New York: Bantam, 1987), 135.
2. Ibid., 136.
3. Information on sheep and shepherding is taken from Phillip Keller's book *A Shepherd Looks at the Good Shepherd and His Sheep* (Grand Rapids: Zondervan, 1978), 75, 89.
4. Ibid., 115.

Chapter 7—The Lamb of God

1. Adapted and expanded from Francis A. Schaeffer, *Death in the City* (Downers Grove, Ill.: InterVarsity Press, 1969), 112–13.
2. Robert Lowry, "Nothing but the Blood," in *Gospel Music,* William Doane and Robert Lowry (New York: Biglow & Main, 1876).

3. To read more about this fascinating correlation, see Edward Chumney, *The Seven Festivals of the Messiah* (Shippensburg, Penn.: Treasure House, 1994), 44–46.

Chapter 8—The Miracle That Changed the World

1. Wilbur M. Smith, *Therefore, Stand: A Plea for a Vigorous Apologetic in the Present Crisis of Evangelical Christianity* (Boston: W. A. Wilde Company, 1945), 362.
2. Philip Schaff, *History of the Christian Church,* vol. 1 (Peabody, Mass.: Hendrickson Publishers, 1996), 172.
3. The stories of the people from Russia, Canada, and Borneo recount just a few of the people touched by the *JESUS* film. Paul Eshleman, *The Touch of Jesus* (Orlando: NewLife Publications, 1995), 243–44, 172, 115–16.
4. This material, including the chart, comes from Bill Bright, *First Love: Renewing Your Passion for God* (Orlando: NewLife Publications, 2002), 39.

Chapter 9—Christ in Me

1. Becky Hill, "Outlook," *Worldwide Challenge* 29, no. 3 (May/June 2002): 8.
2. Howard Hardegree, "A Hot Topic," *Worldwide Challenge* 29, no. 3 (May/June 2002): 13.
3. Howard Hardegree, "Anything but Ordinary," *Worldwide Challenge* 29, no. 6 (November/December 2002): 34–35.
4. To read more about the concept of spiritual breathing, see Bill Bright, *Have You Made the Wonderful Discovery of the Spirit-filled Life?* (Orlando: NewLife Publications, 1966).

Chapter 10—The Love of Jesus

1. Howard Hardegree, "Life and Death in Paradise," *Worldwide Challenge* 30, no. 1 (January–February 2003): 42.
2. Bill Bright, *How You Can Love by Faith* (Orlando: NewLife Publications, 1998).
3. Corrie ten Boom with John and Elizabeth Sherrill, *The Hiding Place* (Washington Depot, Conn.: Chosen, 1971), 187.
4. Ibid., 190.
5. If you want to learn more about loving by faith, read Bill Bright, *How You Can Love by Faith* (Orlando: NewLife Publications, 1998).

Chapter 11—The Leadership of Jesus

1. Read the biblical account of this story in John 13:1–17.
2. Paul Eshleman, *The Touch of Jesus* (Orlando: NewLife Publications, 1995), 149–56.

Chapter 12—The Obedience of Jesus

1. JoAnne Cramberg, "Tulsa's 'Bad Boy' Gary Busey Accepts Jesus," *Connection Magazine* (December 1997); see also <http://www.connectionmagazine.org/badboy.htm>.

Chapter 13—The Prayers of Jesus

1. Elizabeth Bahe, "Modern Art," *Worldwide Challenge* 29, no. 5 (September/ October 2002): 12–19.

Chapter 14—The Body of Christ

1. Joel L. Swerdlow, "Quiet Miracles of the Brain," *National Geographic* (June 1995): 6–19.
2. Jeff Struecker with Elizabeth Bahe, "Beyond *Black Hawk Down,*" *Worldwide Challenge* 30, no. 1 (January/February 2003): 20–21.

Chapter 15—The Mission of Jesus

1. Jennifer Abegg, "One Year Later," *Worldwide Challenge* 29, no. 5 (September/ October 2002): 39–40.
2. Chuck Price with Ron Londen, "An Open Window," *Worldwide Challenge* 29, no. 1 (January/February 2002): 28.
3. *Our Daily Bread* (Grand Rapids: Radio Bible Class Ministries), February 4, 1994.
4. Adapted from an illustration originally published in *Leadership Journal.* Used by permission of Rusty Stephens.

Chapter 16—A Savior Who Never Fails

1. To read more about the contract and vision, see Michael Richardson's book *Amazing Faith: The Authorized Biography of Bill Bright* (Colorado Springs, Colo.: WaterBrook Press, 2000).
2. To read more about God's promises to us in the midst of Satan's attacks, see Bill Bright's book *Promises: A Daily Guide to Supernatural Living* (Orlando: NewLife Publications, 1993), 174.
3. To read more about God's promises to us in our stages of life, see *Promises,* 287.
4. James S. Stewart, *Heralds of God* (New York: C. Scribner's Sons, 1946).

ABOUT THE AUTHOR

DR. BILL BRIGHT, fueled by his passion to share the love and claims of Jesus Christ with "every living person on earth," was the founder and president of Campus Crusade for Christ (CCC). The world's largest Christian ministry, CCC serves people in 191 countries through a staff of 26,000 full-time employees and more than 225,000 trained volunteers working in some 60 targeted ministries and projects ranging from military ministry to inner-city ministry.

Bill Bright was so motivated by what is known as the Great Commission, Christ's command to carry the gospel throughout the world, that in 1956 he wrote a booklet titled *The Four Spiritual Laws,* which has been printed in 200 languages and distributed to more than 2.5 billion people, making it the most widely disseminated religious booklet in history. Other books Bright wrote include *Discover the Book God Wrote, God: Discover His Character, Come Help Change Our World, The Holy Spirit: The Key to Supernatural Living, Life without Equal, Witnessing without Fear, Coming Revival, Journey Home,* and *Red Sky in the Morning.*

In 1979 Bright commissioned the *JESUS* film, a feature-length documentary on the life of Christ. The film has been viewed by more than 5.7 billion people in 191 countries and has become the most widely viewed and translated film in history.

Dr. Bright died in July 2003 before the final editing of this book. But he prayed that it would leave a legacy of his love for Jesus and the power of the Holy Spirit to change lives. He is survived by his wife, Vonette, their sons and daughters-in-law, as well as four grandchildren.

From the Heart of Bill Bright

THE LEGACY SERIES

When Bill Bright, the founder of Campus Crusade for Christ, passed away on July 19, 2003, he was in the middle of writing two books and working on a study Bible. The book you hold in your hand is a collection of the final thoughts Bill Bright had about Jesus Christ—the Person who changed Bill's life forever.

Tyndale House Publishers proudly announces the publication of the other book Bill Bright was working on before he died: *Discover the Book God Wrote*. In it Bill answers questions about the book he loved the most. Study guides and step-by-step instructions help any reader understand the Bible, the book that changed Bill Bright's life—and will change yours as well.

Look for *Discover the Book God Wrote* wherever fine books are sold.

Also, look for *The Discover God Study Bible*. Coming in 2006

The Discover God team, drawn together by Bill Bright, has committed to continue Bill Bright's vision of creating a study Bible that can help people discover God and His will for their lives.

Go to www.discoverGod.org for more information about the Discover God movement and Discover God small groups.